W9-AZG-437

Slaves Who Dared
The Stories of Ten African-American Heroes

By

Mary Garrison

WHITE MANE KIDS
SHIPPENSBURG, PENNSYLVANIA

This White Mane Books publication
was printed by
Beidel Printing House, Inc.
63 West Burd Street
Shippensburg, PA 17257-0708 USA

The acid-free paper used in this book meets the guidelines for permanence and durability of the Committee on Production Guidelines for Book Longevity of the Council on Library Resources.

For a complete list of available publications
please write
White Mane Books
Division of White Mane Publishing Company, Inc.
P.O. Box 708
Shippensburg, PA 17257-0708 USA

Library of Congress Cataloging-in-Publication Data
Garrison, Mary, 1952–
    Slaves who dared : the stories of ten African-American heroes / by Mary Garrison.
      p. cm.
    Summary: Describes the lives and times of outstanding African Americans who were born as slaves and went on to accomplish great things: Josiah Henson, Frederick Douglas, William and Ellen Craft, Harriet Ann Jacobs, Henry Bibb, Booker T. Washington, Susie King Taylor, Nat Love, Robert Smalls, and Sojourner Truth.
    Includes bibliographical references and index.
    ISBN 1-57249-272-4 (alk. paper)
    1. Slaves--United States--Biography--Juvenile literature. 2. Heroes--United States--Biography--Juvenile literature. 3. African Americans--Biography--Juvenile literature. [1. Slaves. 2. Heroes. 3. Slavery. 4. African Americans--Biography.] I. Title

E444 .G37 2002
973'.0496073'00922--dc21
    [B]   2002022666

PRINTED IN THE UNITED STATES OF AMERICA

In memory
of
Webb Garrison
friend, mentor, and father-in-law
(July 19, 1919–July 20, 2000)

Contents

Acknowledgments vi

Introduction vii

Chapter 1 The Slave Who Inspired *Uncle Tom's Cabin*
Josiah Henson (1789–1882) 1

Chapter 2 From Slave to Presidential Advisor
Frederick Douglass (1818–1895) 13

Chapter 3 Masters of Disguise
William and Ellen Craft (1826–1891) 26

Chapter 4 Slave Girl in the Attic
Harriet Ann Jacobs (1813–1897) 38

Chapter 5 Freedom or Family
Henry Bibb (1815–1854) 49

Chapter 6 The Most Famous Black Man in America
Booker T. Washington (1856–1915) 61

Chapter 7 A Woman in the Regiment
Susie King Taylor (1848–1912) 74

Chapter 8 Deadwood Dick and the Wild, Wild West
Nat Love (1854–1925) 91

Chapter 9 Runaway on the Water
Robert Smalls (1839–1915) 103

Chapter 10 A Woman of Truth
Sojourner Truth (1797–1883) 118

Suggested Reading 131

Bibliography 133

Index 139

Acknowledgments

- To Bill for his computer skills, never-ending patience and support.
- To all family members and friends who read, researched, and suggested.
- To the Avery Research Center for African-American History and Culture—College of Charleston, South Carolina; North Carolina Archives and History, University of North Carolina-Chapel Library, University of North Carolina-Charlotte Library; East Carolina University Library; South Caroliniana Library—University of South Carolina, and South Carolina State Library.
- To the University of North Carolina-Chapel Hill for providing the public with online slave narratives. Visit this valuable research site, Documenting the American South, at http://metalab.unc.edu/document.

Introduction

Think about the last time you went to the store to buy something. You walked in and looked at your choices considering size, color, and price. Finally you made a decision. Next, you went to the cash register and put down your money. The sales clerk handed you a receipt listing what you bought and the price.

As you walked out of the store, you were the owner of that item. Legally, that purchase was your personal property. It would be against the law for someone to take it away. But, if you tired of it, or you needed the money, you could sell it.

What if the item you just purchased was a person? Wait. You cannot buy people. Can you?

It is hard to imagine a time when people owned other people. As barbaric as this sounds to us today, the practice of slavery lasted for over 200 years in the United States—from 1619 to 1865. When laws were finally passed outlawing the ownership of another human being, there were nearly 4 million enslaved people in our country.

What was it like for children growing up under slave laws? Was there any family life with mothers, fathers, brothers and sisters? Were children sold or just adults? Did enslaved people have any rights?

There is no way to fully answer these questions unless we lived through the experience ourselves. Fortunately, we do have the written words of brave men and women who were once enslaved. Years and years ago, they recorded their memories in life stories called slave narratives. Some wrote their memories themselves. Others told their stories aloud and friends wrote for them. Through their powerful words, we can begin to understand what their struggles were like.

Many risked their lives. They were forbidden to read and write, but their thirst for learning was greater than any laws. They refused to accept the unacceptable.

They stole books, traded food for reading lessons, and sneaked into illegal classrooms in churches and homes.

Men and women fell in love and married though that was not legal either. They brought their children into the world because they wanted to live in families. They did this knowing one day they might face the worst danger of all: the slave trader. At any moment, owners could decide to sell a slave—for slaves were considered personal property. Countless families were split apart, never to meet again.

Many slaves were mistreated, underfed, and poorly clothed. Some were cruelly whipped over and over. Others just could not bear the thought of being owned when they knew it was against God's laws. As former slave Henry Bibb put it, "The voice of liberty was thundering in my very soul, 'Be free, oh man, be free.'"

Some could not bear the pain any longer, and they decided to run even if it meant death. Once free, these men and women often returned to rescue other slaves and family members. Many became speakers for the anti-slavery societies. Others dedicated their lives to ending this cruel practice that was degrading to people of all colors.

Why is it important for young people today to learn about slavery? There are several reasons. First, it has been said that character is born of hardship. Today's young readers have many lessons to learn from those that not only lived their lives with courage under terrible circumstances, but also made lasting contributions in spite of their suffering. Second, though former slaves describe some owners as kind and some as brutally cruel, slavery was wrong. It was a terrible social evil and our nation's economy was strongly tied to it in 1860. The arguments about slavery erupted in a Civil War that nearly tore our country in two. Over 600,000 soldiers died in this conflict.

Third, we should never forget. This was not a pretty time in our nation's history, and some would rather forget slavery ever happened. But it did, and we cannot ignore it. Is it not better to face the past and use that knowledge to help us improve the present? Whether we like it or not, history is a series of building blocks and we have an opportunity to learn from this important time in the life of our country.

In the following pages, read about ten slaves who dared to risk their lives for freedom. Each chapter is based on the facts we know and the very words that the slaves recorded over 100 years ago. (Although Robert Smalls did not write a slave narrative, the facts are recorded in newspapers, biographies, and accounts from his acquaintances and relatives.)

The ten who dared are Josiah Henson, Frederick Douglass, Susie King Taylor, Booker T. Washington, William and Ellen Craft, Harriet Ann Jacobs, Nat Love, Robert Smalls, and Sojourner Truth.

Get ready to meet them. They were real people and they have a story to tell.

Chapter 1

The Slave Who Inspired *Uncle Tom's Cabin* *Josiah Henson (1789-1882)*

With each blow of the hammer, Josiah Henson's father screamed louder and louder. His entire body flinched with pain like he never felt before. The slaves from nearby plantations were there, called together by their owners to see him punished. Many of them stared at the ground, unable to watch. In all his years as a slave, he never experienced anything so cruel. He could not believe this was really happening to him. The white man was slowly nailing his ear to the whipping post.

At that moment, he realized how dearly he would pay for his crime. He did what he thought any man should do. When he saw the overseer attacking his wife, he fought him in a murderous rage. He would have killed him if his wife had not stopped him.

As he discovered, a slave was not just any man. He had committed the worst crime he could commit—striking a white man. The fact that his wife was being hurt did not matter. The big, strong blacksmith named Hewes gave him his punishment: 100 lashes with a leather whip.

The sounds of the whip lashing across his back rang through the air again and again. It tore into his flesh and the blood ran freely. His terrible shrieks and cries could be heard almost a mile away. After 50 strokes, the men checked for a pulse. They decided to give him another 50 even though his back was already raw.

When he came stumbling home, Josiah's father fell to the ground. The side of his face and his back were covered in blood. His ear was no longer there. At the end of his whipping, they cut it off.

Young Josiah Henson was not yet 5 years old when this terrible tragedy happened. His father never recovered from the trauma. In his family, he had always been a lighthearted person, making music on his banjo for them and the other slaves. Now he turned surly and angry. Not long after his beating, his father's owner sold him to an Alabama slave trader. His family never heard from him again.

Another terrible trauma awaited young Josiah not long after this one. Unlike his father's owner, his owner, Dr. Josiah McPherson, was kind, as slave owners go. He never let anyone strike his slaves. Josiah was even named for him. He and his family had a few happy years together on his farm in Charles County, Maryland. But the good doctor liked to drink. One evening he wandered into a creek while drunk and drowned.

Dr. McPherson probably never meant for Josiah's family to be separated. Like many slave owners in the South, he never put in writing what he wanted for his slaves when he died. So after his death, all of his belongings were sold at auction.

One by one, Josiah watched his brothers and sisters go up for sale. Each one went to a different place. His mother's heart was breaking as she said goodbye to all of her children. His mother went to the auction block next. Isaac Riley of nearby Montgomery County bought her. She could not stand the strain a minute more. She threw herself at his feet, grabbed his knees, and begged him to buy her youngest child, Josiah, so she could be with at least one of her children.

> Enslaved people were considered **personal property** under the law. If their owner died, they could be sold just like farm tools or cattle to help pay their owner's debts.

This request was met with blows and kicks and outrage. Josiah said he always remembered the way his mother looked as she crawled away. In his autobiography, he wrote:

> Common as are slave-auctions in the southern states, the misery of the event is never understood till the actual experiences comes. The first sad announcement that the sale is to be; the frantic terror at the idea of being sent 'down south'; the almost certainty that one member of a family will be torn from another; the agony at parting forever with husband, wife, child—these must be seen and felt to be fully understood. Young as I was then, the iron entered my soul.

Josiah was sold to a man named Robb, who stuck him in the slave cabins and forgot all about him. No one there took an interest in looking after a homesick little 5-year-old boy. He soon lost weight and became very sick. His new owner decided to get rid of him and traded him back to Mr. Riley. He was very lucky to be with his mother again.

Josiah's father was well known for his banjo playing. After his owner beat him and cut off his ear, he was never the same man. He was sold and his family never saw him again.

Like Josiah's family members, these people were sold at auction. Many never reunited.

TO BE SOLD, on board the Ship *Bance Island*, on tuesday the 6th of *May* next, at *Ashley-Ferry*, a choice cargo of about 250 fine healthy

NEGROES,

just arrived from the Windward & Rice Coast. —The utmost care has already been taken, and shall be continued, to keep them free from the least danger of being infected with the SMALL-POX, no boat having been on board, and all other communication with people from *Charles-Town* prevented.

Austin, Laurens, & Appleby.

N. B. Full one Half of the above Negroes have had the SMALL-POX in their own Country.

An advertisement for a slave auction

Josiah was a smart young man and full of curiosity. He was interested in learning to read even though it was forbidden. He was respected by the other slaves too. Mr. Riley often put him in charge because of this. Sometimes, Josiah took extra food to give to some of the slaves. He never felt like this was stealing because they worked so hard and their owner never fed them enough.

As a teenager, Josiah learned of a minister, John McKenny, who preached just a few miles from his home. He got up his nerve to ask Mr. Riley if he could attend one of his sermons. His mother was a religious woman, teaching her children the Lord's Prayer. Riley let him go to the service that turned out to be an important moment in his life. The sermon focused on God's love for everyone, slave or free. This got Josiah interested in preaching, which he soon began to do for the slave community.

Josiah became a more and more responsible worker. Riley allowed him to go alone to market in Washington, D.C., to sell goods from the farm. On his trips, he observed the speech and habits of the townspeople. When Josiah was 18, Riley decided to save some money and let him be in charge of the slaves, instead of hiring an overseer.

Around this time, Josiah met a young woman named Charlotte and they fell in love. They married in a "jumping the broom" ceremony. Over the years, they had four sons, Tom, Isaac, Peter, and little Josiah.

> Enslaved people had **no rights** under the law. Their marriages were not recognized, and they were not allowed to read and write. They could not testify against white men in court. They were at the mercy of their owners.

Soon, Josiah became Riley's most trusted slave. He took him everywhere, even to his Saturday night cockfights. One night, the crowd got rowdier than usual and Riley got into a fight with an overseer named Bruce Litton. In the midst of the struggle, Riley called for Josiah's help. When jumping into the fight, Josiah tripped Litton, who had a nasty, mean side.

Later that week, Josiah met up with Bruce Litton and three of his slaves. Litton ordered his workers to hold Josiah as he beat him with a fence rail. He broke and crushed both of his shoulder blades. No doctor was ever called to set the bones, and Josiah was unable to lift his arms above his head for the rest of his life.

Times were hard, and Mr. Riley had financial trouble. He realized that his farm and his slaves were going to be taken away from him so he could pay his bills. Riley decided that he did not want to lose his slaves, so he sent them to his brother, Amos, in Kentucky.

Riley chose Josiah to lead the group of 18 to their new home. Along the way, they crossed into a "free" state. Companions on the road urged them to run away. Josiah thought long and hard about it and knew he made a promise. He convinced the group to go on to Kentucky. Later, he realized he made a terrible mistake. The new owner soon sold many of his friends. He was haunted by this the rest of his life.

Josiah began to think about buying his freedom. A friend, a white Methodist minister, convinced him to earn money by preaching. The minister told Josiah to tell Amos

> Before the Civil War, our country was deeply divided. Slavery was allowed in some states, and not in others. These states were referred to as **free states** and **slave states.** Arguments over this issue led to the outbreak of war.

that he wanted to go visit Mr. Riley in Maryland. Along the way, Josiah earned $250. When he arrived in Maryland, Riley agreed to give Josiah his freedom for $450, so Josiah sold his horse for $100 and combined that with the $250 he had earned while en route. Riley made Josiah promise to pay the additional $100 as soon as he earned it; the freedom papers were then drawn up and sent with Josiah back to Kentucky.

> Freedom papers for enslaved people were also called **manumission papers.**

When Amos opened up the freedom papers from his brother, he read them to Josiah. Riley had tricked him! The price had been changed to $1,000. No longer did Josiah feel obligated to play the role of loyal slave. He planned to run away.

Amos and Isaac began arguing over who really owned Josiah. So, they decided to sell him. On the trip down the river, Amos became seriously ill. He begged Josiah to take care of him and get him safely back home. Josiah did but he knew it was time to get serious. The next time they decided to sell him he might not be so lucky.

At the first opportunity, Josiah and his family slipped away in a boat at night with the help of a friend. Charlotte was terrified of being caught. She begged to stay behind with the children.

Josiah insisted the whole family come. He carried his two youngest sons on his back in a handmade sling for most of the 600-mile journey. The family heard the way to freedom was by reading the night sky.

They slept during the day in the woods and by night they walked. At one point they

> Today, it is hard to imagine going on a long, dangerous journey without a map or directions. Yet thousands of enslaved people found their way to freedom by following the **North Star** in the evening sky. The destination for many runaways was Canada, where slavery was outlawed.

ran out of food. Josiah took a chance and went begging for food. A kind woman gave him venison and bread. They had no cups to drink from, so they used their father's shoes. He said in his autobiography that they enjoyed this food and drink more than any meal they ever had together as a family.

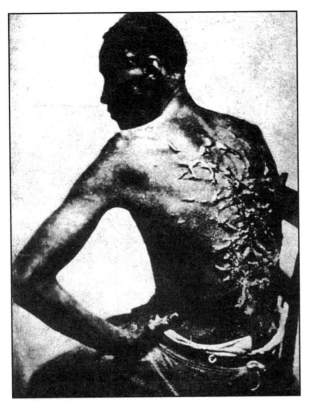

Like Josiah's father, this man was whipped by his owner. There were no laws protecting black people from such cruel treatment.

National Archives

Josiah was trusted to lead a group of slaves to Kentucky. He persuaded them to not run away when they crossed into a free state. Later he deeply regretted this when his owner sold many of his friends.

Library of Congress

With the help of Indians and a Scottish boatman, the family safely arrived in Canada. Josiah said:

(I) threw myself on the ground, rolled in the sand, seized handfuls of it and kissed them, and danced around, till, in the eyes of several who were present, I passed for a madman. "He's some crazy fellow," said Colonel Warren who happened to be there. "Oh no, master! Don't you know? I'm free!"

Immediately, Josiah and his family went to work. They farmed for a Mr. Hibbard, who gave them a crude house to live in. Within three years, Josiah owned pigs, cows, and a horse. He also started preaching in his new community. Mr. Hibbard realized that Josiah's son Tom was very bright and arranged for him to go to school. After Tom learned to read and write, he taught Josiah.

Many other free black men and escaped slaves lived nearby. Soon they formed an association to buy or to rent property together. Some of the families, hearing of Josiah's bravery in bringing his family to freedom, begged him to rescue their family members. Josiah thought this over for a long time and decided he should do whatever he could to help his fellow man. He became an agent of the Underground Railroad and rescued 118 people during his lifetime.

Josiah and other fugitive slaves eventually bought property and started their own town, which they named Dawn. One of the prides of his life was the school they founded there. It was first called the Manual Labour Institution, and friends in England donated money to support it. It operated on a work and study plan. The students were taught practical skills in addition to reading and writing. Although the school had few students at first, people soon begged to get in. The town grew as a blacksmith shop and gristmill were added. The citizens planned to raise funds for a sawmill too.

> The **Underground Railroad** was the name given to a group of very brave people. They took dangerous risks to feed, hide or transport runaways. Some of them were free blacks, and some were enslaved. White men and women helped too. They lived in many different states and used code words. **Conductors and agents** led and moved runaways from hiding place to hiding place called **stations. Harriet Tubman** was called the Moses of her people. A former slave herself, she led 300 people to freedom. **Levi Coffin**, a white man from Pennsylvania, assisted 3,000 escapees.

About this time, Josiah's popularity as a preacher increased. He was eventually assigned a 300-mile district as a Methodist minister. He seemed to have the right ingredients. He had a pleasant personality, a good sense of humor, and he got along well with most people. Soon, he traveled to the New England states to preach for the anti-slavery society. He began to realize that many people in the North were afraid to oppose slavery. The Northern economy depended on the cotton from the South. Most workers in the North worked for textile mills that used this cotton.

Through his speeches, Josiah was able to make people there realize how terrible slavery was. In 1849, he wrote his story in a small 26-page book called *The Life of Josiah Henson, Formerly a Slave.* When he wrote this book, he had no idea how important it would become.

The next year, a very serious young woman visited the offices of the Massachusetts Anti-Slavery Society. Her name was Harriet Beecher Stowe. One of the things she read there was Josiah's book and it made a big impression on her. It only proved to her what she imagined slave life would be like from the things she saw in her own town.

Harriet lived in Cincinnati, Ohio, a place where many runaways stopped on their journey to freedom. There she often saw the terrible treatment the slaves received when the slave hunters found them and took them back across the river. She was troubled for years about this. Around the same time, Harriet's son became very ill and died. She said she felt she could appreciate the grief of any mother losing her child.

In 1850, Josiah was on a speaking tour. Harriet heard about it and asked him to visit her at her brother's home. In his later writings he spoke about this meeting. She asked many questions about the story of his life. During their visit, he told her many details about growing up and she was very sympathetic. Harriet told him she was glad he had written his book so other people could understand why slavery must be stopped.

Long after the visit was over, Harriet continued to think about Josiah and the terrible things that had happened to him.

Harriet Beecher Stowe, the famous author of Uncle Tom's Cabin. *Some historians consider her book the most influential in American history. She wrote about the evils of slavery after meeting Josiah and reading his story.*
Library of Congress

Perhaps the combination of his book and their visit plus the death of her son led Harriet to write. She contacted a newspaper editor of the *National Era* and asked if he would like her to write a series of stories about slavery.

Once she started, there was no stopping Harriet. She submitted chapter after chapter. This went on for 40 weeks. Thousands of readers waited each week for the continuation of her story. People could not wait to find out what happened to Tom, the hero of her story, who was a faithful slave very similar to Josiah Henson. Many of the events and characters were loosely based on his life. A Boston publisher, J. P. Jewett, contacted her about putting her story into a book.

On March 20, 1852, Harriet's book was released. It was called *Uncle Tom's Cabin; or Life Among the Lowly.* Neither Harriet nor Josiah could have predicted what an impact this book would have. This book played an important role in the period leading up to the Civil War. It made the disagreements between people of the North and South even

> The first day out, **Uncle Tom's Cabin** sold 3,000 copies. It went on to sell 500,000 in the next five years. It was translated into 23 languages, and Great Britain printed 1.5 million copies. It is still for sale today.

This child was an important character in Harriet Beecher Stowe's famous book. Citizens in the North became very upset when they read her stories on the suffering of slaves.

Library of Congress

135,000 SETS, 270,000 VOLUMES SOLD.

UNCLE TOM'S CABIN

FOR SALE HERE.

AN EDITION FOR THE MILLION, COMPLETE IN 1 Vol., PRICE 37 1-2 CENTS.
"   "   IN GERMAN, IN 1 Vol., PRICE 50 CENTS.
"   "   IN 2 Vols,. CLOTH, 6 PLATES, PRICE $1.50.
SUPERB ILLUSTRATED EDITION, IN 1 Vol., WITH 153 ENGRAVINGS,
PRICES FROM $2.50 TO $5.00.

The Greatest Book of the Age.

Uncle Tom's Cabin sold 300,000 copies the first year. The story fanned the flames of war between the North and South.

Collection of The New-York Historical Society #38219

stronger than before. Some even said that her book was what caused the start of the war. In fact, some historians say that President Abraham Lincoln made this remark when he met Harriet: "So this is the little woman who made the big war."

Harriet's writing style was very melodramatic and emotional. So, many people in the South disliked her and thought her book was full of lies and exaggeration. She received a lot of hate letters. Once someone mailed her the ear of a black person.

Josiah himself said that

Mrs. Stowe's book was not an exaggerated account of the evils of slavery. The truth has never been half told; the story would be too horrible to bear.

Harriet received so much criticism that she decided to write a key, or explanation about her book, telling where she got her information. She published this 1 year after the book came out. Although she said she never intended her book to be about one particular slave, she said that some events in Josiah's life were used for her character Uncle Tom. Everywhere Josiah went after this, he was called "Uncle Tom."

Eliza and child, runaway slaves

Being young and inexperienced, Harriet did not take the proper steps to protect her book from being misused. All over the country, there were plays called "Tom shows". Instead of showing Tom as he was in her book or Josiah's story, he became a clownish, ridiculous character who did what he was told. Today, calling a black man an "Uncle Tom" is an insult. It means they do not have the courage to stand up for themselves. Josiah Henson was anything but what we all an Uncle Tom today. Still, the name has stayed with him. He wrote in his autobiography:

> I have been called "Uncle Tom" and I feel proud of the title. If my humble words in any way inspired that gifted lady to write such a plaintive story that the whole community has been touched with pity for the sufferings of the poor slave, I have not lived in vain.

Josiah went on to republish his story in a book called *Truth Stranger than Fiction*. With money from the sales, he was able to buy his long-lost brother's freedom and to take him to Canada. When the sawmill in Dawn, Canada, was in trouble, Josiah went to England to the Great Exposition to take orders for their fine walnut wood. Queen Victoria stopped briefly at his booth to look. On another visit to England, he was invited to visit the Queen at Windsor Castle so she could meet the real Uncle Tom. She gave him a photograph of her, which he hung in his home in Canada.

The next year, Josiah decided to visit Maryland and Washington. He was getting older and hoped to see his old home. Frederick Douglass wrote to President and Mrs. Rutherford B. Hayes for Josiah. The Hayes gladly welcomed them for a visit to the White House. Josiah even found his former owner, Mrs. Riley, now in old age, on the farm where he lived as a young boy.

Josiah lived a long, productive life and died at age 93. He was the father of 8 children. In his lifetime, he went from loyal slave to runaway, Methodist Episcopal minister, abolitionist, and writer. He also became an Underground Railroad agent, town organizer, school founder, distinguished traveler and celebrity. What a list of accomplishments this is from the young boy who was crippled by an overseer. His bones were broken but never his spirit.

The Canadian home where Josiah lived for so many years operates today as Uncle Tom's Cabin and Museum in Dresden, Ontario. Here school children from around the country can come learn about Josiah Henson's remarkable life and the story of the Underground Railroad. Copies of his original 26-page life story are for sale in the gift shop right along with *Uncle Tom's Cabin*.

For more information about visiting Uncle Tom's Cabin Historic Site, write to RR5, St. Clair Parkway Commission, Dresden, Ontario, Canada, NOP 1MO, or call 519-683-2978. Tour guides are available for school groups.

Josiah became known as the real Uncle Tom after Harriet Beecher Stowe wrote her famous book. She used many episodes from his life story in her book.
Author's Personal Collection

No longer enslaved, Josiah Henson poses with his wife. Josiah's first wife, Charlotte, died after they escaped to Canada. He later married a widow whom he met in Boston.
National Afro-American Museum

Chapter 2

From Slave to Presidential Advisor
Frederick Douglass (1818–1895)

Fred Bailey heard approaching footsteps. He was only 5 or 6 years old, but he recognized the footsteps of Captain Anthony. Fred's Aunt Hester and her boyfriend, Ned, had been visiting near the small town of Tuckahoe, Maryland. Fred knew this was against plantation rules in Eaton County. It was the 1820s, and slaves had no rights except those given to them by their owners.

Carrying a cowhide whip, Anthony burst into the cabin and stripped off Aunt Hester's clothing to her waist. He made her cross her hands, then tied them together. Soon she was suspended from a big hook in the ceiling. Writing much later, Fred recalled that "After rolling up his sleeves he commenced to lay on the heavy cowskin. Amid heart-rending shrieks from her and horrid oaths from him, soon the warm, red blood came dripping to the floor."

Little Fred was so terrified that he hid in a closet and began thinking that it would be his turn to get the next whipping. That's when he began to know what it meant to be the property of someone else. He was very small, but he made up his mind he wouldn't spend his whole life enslaved. At the time, he didn't dream that he would grow up to become an advisor to President Abraham Lincoln.

Fred's grandmother picked his name—Frederick Augustus Washington Bailey. He never knew the date of his birth and didn't know his father's name. Later in life he realized that his father was probably a white man—maybe Captain Anthony.

In Maryland, slave owners often moved mothers to nearby plantations when their babies were quite young. Fred remembered only 4 or 5 visits from his mother,

On many plantations, a cabin served as the kitchen. Fred slept in the kitchen closet as a young boy. He hid there when Captain Anthony burst in and viciously whipped his Aunt Hester.

Library of Congress

always at night. When he was 7, his mother became ill and died. Since Fred lived on a different plantation, he learned about this later. He was not allowed to go to her funeral.

After he grew up, Fred told the story of his life, and friends helped him write his memories. From this we know that the person he loved the most was his grandmother, Betsy Bailey. Most slave families lived in small, crowded shacks. Grandmother Betsy had her own cabin away from the others. As she was too old to work in the fields, it was her job to tend the children while the mothers worked.

A **plantation** was a very large farm that raised crops like cotton or tobacco. Many were like small villages with their own stables and blacksmith shops. It took many people to run a plantation. Some had hundreds of workers.

As Fred grew older, he realized his life was different from the lives of white children. Someone owned him, his grandmother, and her house. One day, his grandmother told him, he would go to the big plantation to live with the older children. He would also meet his owner.

Perhaps his grandmother meant well, but she never told him the reason for their trip one sunny day. She simply left him with a group of playing children at Col. Edward Lloyd's plantation, his new home. After crying for some time, Fred adjusted to his new life. There was not much work for young children to do until age 7 or 8. So,

The Great House of a Louisiana plantation

Library of Congress

Fred ran errands, helped drive the cattle, and went bird hunting with his owner's young son Daniel.

Like all the younger slaves, his only clothing was a shirt that hung to his knees. Fred had no shoes. Shoes, pants, and jackets were saved for the adult workers. Fred remembered frostbite cracks in his feet deep enough to put a writing pen inside. He said that

> **Slave owners** instructed their slaves to call them **Master** and their wives **Mistress.** The owner, his wife, and even his children expected obedience at all times.

> The children unable to work in the field had neither shoes, stockings, jackets, nor trousers given to them; their clothing consisted of two coarse linen shirts per year. When these failed them, they went naked until the next allowance day. Children from seven to ten years old, of both sexes, almost naked, might be seen at all seasons of the year.

Often Fred and his brothers and sisters were hungry. Each adult was regularly allowanced, which meant they were given 8 pounds of pork or fish and a bushel of corn meal to last for a month. But it was never enough especially for those who worked hard all day in the fields. In his autobiography, Fred wrote that

> Children were not regularly allowanced. Our food was coarse corn meal boiled. This was called mush. It was put into a large wooden tray or trough, and set down upon the ground. The children were then called, like so many pigs, and like so many pigs they would come and devour the mush; some with oyster-shells, others with pieces of shingle, some with naked hands, and none with spoons. He that ate fastest got most; he that was strongest secured the best place; and few left the trough satisfied.

At night, Fred was cold. He was smart enough to steal old corn bags to sleep in and stay warmer. Only the adults were given blankets, and there were no beds for the hard clay floors. Even though they were exhausted, everyone was expected to be up early. Anyone late to the fields received a whipping.

Fred soon learned that workers at the Great House had a better food and clothing allowance. Those working in the fields of wheat, corn, and tobacco had the hardest lives of all. They had to worry about the overseer, the man in charge of the slaves in the

> **The Great House or Big House** was the home of the slave owner. Many of these homes were large and beautiful. People who worked there were called **house servants.** Those who worked the crops were known as **field hands.** Slave labor made many white planters wealthy.

fields. He had a whip and he used it whenever he wanted to. Even the owner could punish them for the smallest reason.

Library of Congress

Fred remembered:

> I have seen Col. Lloyd make old Barney, a man between fifty and sixty years of age, uncover his bald head, kneel upon the damp, cold ground and receive upon his naked and toil-worn shoulders more than thirty lashes at a time.

Anyone caught stealing or being disruptive was whipped and put on the owner's ship to Baltimore to be sold.

Mr. Gore, the overseer, became angry one day with a worker named Demby. Gore whipped him, but Demby ran into the creek and would not come out. The overseer threatened to kill him if he did not come out and get the rest of his whipping. Demby just stood there and the overseer killed him with his pistol. He told Colonel Lloyd that he had to set an example. There were no laws protecting enslaved people in cases like this. If an overseer or owner killed a slave, nothing was done.

When he was 8 years old, Colonel Lloyd sent Fred to Baltimore to work for the Auld family. For the journey, Fred received his first pair of pants and a good scrubbing from the other slaves. City slaves were different from plantation slaves, they told him.

> **An overseer** was in charge of the workers in the field. Some overseers were cruel, and beat or tortured the slaves. There were no laws to protect enslaved blacks.

Fred moved to the big city of Baltimore when he was 8.

Frank Leslie's *Our Soldier in the Civil War*

Living conditions in his new home were greatly improved. His new mistress, Mrs. Sophia Auld, was kind and saw that Fred had plenty of food and clothes. She had never been in charge of a slave before and was unaware of the rules most owners used. She decided to teach Fred his ABCs.

Mr. Hugh Auld, her husband, put a stop to that. He said it was against the law to teach a slave to read and write, and only made them unhappy with their lives. But his real worry was those who could read and write often ran away to freedom in Northern states and Canada.

Fred received just enough learning to make him want more. In teaching Fred the alphabet, Mrs. Auld had given him a taste. He was going to have more no matter what it took. He found old books in the house and hid them. He learned that some white children playing in the streets were not as well fed as he was. He stuffed extra bread and food in his pockets and traded that for reading lessons.

The book *The Columbian Orator* had a big influence on Fred. In it he read about slaves who ran away from their owners. He dreamed of freedom and of escaping to the North where all people were free. In the Baltimore shipyards, he learned to write. He challenged other boys to a writing contest. He always lost, but each time he came away with a new word to practice writing.

What happened to Fred next was the hardest part of his life while enslaved. His owners died and by law Fred had to return home to the plantation. All the people and animals were divided up. The families were split up or sold. His grandmother had tended her owner when he was a baby and been at his side when he died. In spite of that

> She was nevertheless left a slave....in the hand of strangers; and in their hands she saw her children, her grandchildren and her great-grandchildren, divided up like so many sheep....her present owner finding she was but of little value, her frame already wracked with the pains of old age,...took her to the woods, built her a little hut, put up a little mud-chimney and then made her support herself there in loneliness....turning her out to die.

Fred was sent to Mr. Thomas Auld's plantation. He and his wife were cruel and let their slaves go hungry. This new owner was mean and beat him often. Finally, he sent Fred to live with Mr. Edward Covey, known as a slave-breaker. He was willing to use any method no matter how vicious to make slaves obey their owners.

The first day, Fred accidentally lost control of the ox cart and wrecked it against a tree. He received a severe beating. There were many more to come during the next 6 months. Fred's spirit began to break. "I was sometimes prompted to take my life and that of Covey," he said.

One day in the field, Fred became sick from the heat and could not stand up. Mr. Covey beat him, kicked him, and then hit him on the head. With blood running from his wound, Fred walked home to his owner for help but he sent him back. On his return, Mr. Covey trapped Fred in the stable and tried to tie him up. Fred wrote:

> You have seen how a man was made a slave; you shall see how a slave was made a man.... At that moment—from whence came the spirit I don't know—I resolved to fight and...I seized Covey hard by the throat.

In Fred's writings, he said the fight lasted for almost 2 hours. Covey could not get the better of him, and after that he never touched Fred again.

This was a turning point in Fred's life. At the next plantation where he lived, he broke the rules and taught other blacks to read and to write. He planned to run away but his owner found out. Fred was then sent back to his old home in Baltimore. Here he was allowed to work for wages that he saved for his escape. A sailor friend of Fred's gave him his identification papers. He pretended to be the sailor and used his papers to board a train to New York.

It was a dangerous journey and he was almost discovered several times. At that time, slaves in the North could be captured and returned to their owners because of a law called the Fugitive Slave Act. Anyone helping or hiding a slave could be fined or put in prison.

> The **Fugitive Slave Act** was passed in 1850, and runaway slaves were not safe anywhere. Slave owners could travel to the free states to bring them home. Under this law, any person helping slaves escape, hiding them, or trying to stop their capture could be thrown in jail and fined. Although slaves were people, they were treated as pieces of property by law.

Frederick Douglass was the most famous runaway in America.

Library of Congress

Although Fred was in danger, he began a new life with a new name. He was no longer Frederick Augustus Washington Bailey but Frederick Douglass—the name that made him famous across the country and the one studied in our history books today.

In adopting a new name, Frederick Douglass became a new person. He became a very important figure in the years before and during the Civil War. He was a protestor of the unfair laws and practices against black people in the North. His children were not allowed to attend school in the area of town where they lived. There were separate pews in churches. Black passengers could not buy

Fred posed as a sailor and escaped on a train to New York. It was the biggest and busiest city in the nation.

Frederick Douglass, as seen in his slave narrative in 1845. His book helped many Americans understand slavery. Though born as a slave, Douglass became a newspaper editor and a fiery speaker for the anti-slavery societies.

first-class train tickets. On steamships, they were required to stay on deck. Douglass protested and fought until many of these laws were changed.

Frederick Douglass was invited to talk at an Anti-Slavery Convention and was immediately hired as a speaker. He was known to draw crowds as large as 5,000, and was once attacked by a mob. He became the most famous fugitive slave in the country and showed what a free black man could accomplish. After he published his first autobiography, *Narrative of the Life of Frederick Douglass: an American Slave,* he fled to England to hide from his owners. Quaker friends bought his freedom papers so he could return.

Abolitionists were people working to end slavery. They formed anti-slavery societies in the North and helped runaways like Frederick Douglass publish the truth about slavery.

Many people who knew little about slavery read his story. They were outraged. It helped the abolitionists educate people about why slavery should end. Douglass was doing his part by also working for the Underground Railroad, a secret organization that helped slaves run away.

He regularly hid blacks that were on their way to Canada. At one time, he had 11 people hiding in his house. Because of the fugitive slave laws, he could have been fined or sent to prison.

The conflict about slavery between the North and South kept growing. The U.S.

The Underground Railroad was not really underground. It just seemed to the slave owners like runaways must be hiding below the ground when they disappeared. It was not a real railroad either but a group of brave people across the country who felt slavery was wrong. They were willing to risk going to jail to help runaway slaves. Slaves hid in their homes and then got directions to the next safe stop.

Congress had many bitter fights about fugitive slave laws and other matters. The presidential race was very bitter, with angry feelings between those who owned slaves and those who did not. When Mr. Lincoln won, many Southerners were ready to start their own country with their own constitution. When some of them decided to "secede," or withdraw from the United States, war broke out.

Frederick Douglass grew even busier during the war. One of the most important things that Douglass did to help his people was to start a newspaper written by blacks. It was the only newspaper of its kind at the time that was published regularly. Friends from England gave him $2,500 to start it. His paper was called the *North Star* and was later changed to *Frederick Douglass's Paper.* He chose this name because fugitive slaves were told to "follow the North Star" to freedom.

This newspaper educated people about slavery and the work of the abolitionists. It also helped to recruit black soldiers in the middle of the war. At first, the Union army would not let free blacks or fugitive slaves serve as soldiers. The generals even allowed slave hunters to come into their army camps to seize runaways.

After losing many battles, President Lincoln agreed to let black men serve. But for a while they were only allowed to do dirty work instead of fighting. They were also required to wear a different uniform from the other soldiers. Many were paid half wages or sent to work in forts infected with yellow fever.

President Abraham Lincoln got advice from Douglass, but did not seek it from any other former slave.

Library of Congress, Alexander Gardner, Photographer

The president hoped more blacks would come north and serve in the army. Douglass ran ads like these in his newspaper, the **North Star.**

Library of Congress

When the president allowed blacks to serve as soldiers, the *North Star* went to work publishing stories and ads. Douglass helped to find soldiers to serve in the 54th and 55th Massachusetts all-black regiments. These soldiers distinguished themselves in battle at Fort Wagner and proved that black soldiers could do their part. This was a big turning point for black people. After this, black soldiers were used regularly. Douglass's sons Lewis and Charles served as soldiers during the war. Frederick Jr. was a recruiter.

Frederick Douglass was still upset by the unequal treatment of blacks in the army. Their pay was not equal to that of white soldiers, and some were captured and

The black 54th Massachusetts Regiment, led by a white officer, had two sons of Frederick Douglass in its ranks.

Library of Congress

sold into slavery. He decided to go to Washington and invite himself to the White House to discuss this with President Lincoln himself.

This was a very brave act because blacks and whites did not talk on equal terms back then. Black people did not just decide to invite themselves to the White House. But the president agreed to meet Douglass and listen to his complaints. Lincoln thought the problems would be slowly corrected. He agreed to give commissions to any black soldier recommended to him by the secretary of war. A commission was a way to recognize their good work and gave them the same privileges as white soldiers.

After the president made a proclamation freeing the slaves, he invited Douglass back to the White House as an advisor. He was disappointed that more enslaved people had not heard about his proclamation. He hoped more blacks would soon be coming across the enemy lines to claim their freedom. Frederick Douglass promised to help the president spread the word.

The night before President Lincoln's second inauguration, Frederick Douglass was asked to tea with Chief Justice Salmon P. Chase. This was unusual because blacks and whites did not eat at the same table during the Civil War years. After the inauguration, Douglass met with a big disappointment. The inaugural reception was open to the public. He stood in the line with the crowd to congratulate the president.

At the door, policemen stopped him and said no black people were allowed. Frederick insisted that he be allowed inside. He knew Mr. Lincoln would have no such rule. The policemen took him by the arms and acted like they were escorting him in. They tricked him and led him right out the back door.

Frederick spotted a friend in the crowd and had him sneak a message in to the president. Soon Frederick and his companion were admitted. Inside the elegant White House, they shook hands and talked with Abraham Lincoln himself. It turned out that there was no rule forbidding blacks. The police were just acting out of old customs.

Frederick Douglass invited himself to the nation's capital to visit President Lincoln. Here is a familiar Washington building, the U.S. Capitol, before it was finished. Douglass visited the city to convince leaders to let blacks serve as soldiers. Later, he lobbied for equal pay. He also attended the president's inauguration.

Abraham Lincoln often consulted Frederick Douglass. He was the only black man who was an advisor to the President during 1861–65. That gave him a very special place in our history.

If you visit Washington, be sure to see the Frederick Douglass Home, a national historic site. You can learn more about it on the internet at http://www.nps.gov/frdo.

Another important site is the Lincoln Memorial. It has taken the place of a monument to Lincoln that was unveiled in 1876. Douglass made the main speech in ceremonies held then. President Ulysses S. Grant, his cabinet, and members of Congress listened. Thousands of people crowded close in order to hear the speech.

Years later in 1963, Martin Luther King, Jr., led the movement for civil rights for African Americans. In fact, King gave his famous "I Have a Dream" speech near the same spot where Douglass spoke. Along with King, the boy Fred who saw Aunt Hester whipped until she wished she were dead became one of our nation's most famous black citizens.

Salmon P. Chase, U.S. secretary of the treasury, invited Douglass to his home for tea.

Library of Congress

Once a runaway slave, Frederick Douglass became a powerful leader of his people. After the abolition of slavery, he became a U.S. marshal and U.S. minister of Haiti.

Library of Congress

Chapter 3

Masters of Disguise
William and Ellen Craft (1826–1891)

An elderly man sat at the captain's table on a steamship bound for Charleston, South Carolina. He was an ordinary looking old man except for his right hand. It was covered with foul-smelling brown medicine that leaked through a cloth sling. His jaw was tied up in a kerchief, a sure sign of a toothache. Behind his green glasses, he looked rather sickly.

As the white men around the table continued their meal, they took up their favorite topic of discussion: slaves and how to tame them. "You can't be polite," said one. "You must yell and threaten and frighten them. A regular whipping keeps them in line. Then they will be afraid and obey you." Heads around the table nodded as they agreed with the speaker.

As the male servant of the elderly man appeared, a slave trader in the crowd spoke up. "Never, never take a slave up north. If he doesn't run away, he will come back with his head full of escape plans," he preached. "You, sir," he said to the old man whose slave was cutting his meat since his arm was wounded. "How about selling me that boy there? That will stop any ideas of running away."

The crowd of men laughed together. The old man explained that he could not possibly travel without his faithful servant. "You can never trust a slave," exclaimed one of them. As another man gave his opinion, the elderly man just settled back in his chair and listened.

He thought, "What would these men do if they discovered they were dining with a slave wearing lady's bloomers at this very moment." Underneath a disguise as a sickly old man sat Ellen Craft, a runaway slave. She continued to chat with the slave trader as she finished her dinner. On the outside, she looked like an old man. But on the inside, she was quaking with fear. She was a fugitive slave fighting and running for her life.

Four nights earlier in Macon, Georgia, Ellen and her husband, William, had dreamed of escape. As they talked, they came up with a daring plan requiring lies and disguises. If not for the shade of Ellen's skin, they would never have considered the risk. Like many slaves, Ellen's father was a white man—her mother's owner.

When Ellen was growing up, she was often mistaken for white. In fact, her mistress became upset when people called Ellen her daughter. To rid herself of this terribly embarrassing problem, she gave Ellen to a relative when she was 11 years old. In just a few short years, that pale skin would be her ticket to freedom.

William did not have much contact with his parents or brothers and sisters growing up. Once his owner sold them, he never saw them again. When his owner went into debt, William, too, was sold. But, fortunately for him, his cabinet-making skills brought him near the home where Ellen lived. He fell in love and she filled the empty place in his heart his family once occupied. Although they lived nearly 100 miles apart, they decided to marry in a slave ceremony known as "jumping the broom."

As the days and weeks went by, they found it harder and harder to be apart. They dreamed of living together in a place where black men were free. William thought about this idea all the time. As he looked for ways to escape, he thought about how his owner usually took a servant or two on trips. Why could Ellen not pretend to be a slave owner, and he the slave?

When he first told Ellen his plan, she was terrified. She said she could never do it.

Jumping the broom was the name of marriage ceremonies for enslaved people. A couple simply jumped together over a broomstick that lay on the ground. This was a substitute for a true legal ceremony where couples promised to be together until "death do us part." Since slave families were often split apart when sold, they could not make this promise. Besides, the laws of the time did not allow enslaved blacks to marry.

Slave owners on some plantations performed weddings. Sometimes the black preacher wed the couples or the owner called in his own minister. Weddings were a time for celebration including feasting, singing, and dancing. This was a serious ceremony for people even though it was not legally recognized.

As time went on, and the misery of her life away from her husband continued, she felt more hopeful that this idea might work.

The main reason Ellen was so frightened was because pretending to be a slave owner was much harder than it sounded. It was nearly 1,000 miles to freedom! This

Portrait of Ellen Smith Craft
Harriet Tubman Historical and Cultural Museum
Macon, Georgia

meant she had to act for several days, not just a few hours. She would have to make conversation with other white men and to make her voice sound like a man's. Even though she had never learned to read and write, suddenly she would have to speak like an educated gentleman. Would she really be able to make them believe she was a slave owner? If caught, she would be sent back to her owner or even killed.

Traveling also meant she needed to read and write. Like thousands of enslaved people, she could do neither. The laws of the white men made it a crime. Educated slaves were the ones who figured out how to escape. At many train stations, hotels, and customhouses, travelers registered their names and their servants. The brave couple almost cancelled their plan when they realized this. Surely, Ellen would be discovered when asked to write.

Ellen soon thought of a solution. What if she fixed her hand so it could not be used? Then she could ask someone to write for her. Ellen made poultices for both her arm, which she covered with a sling, and her jaw, which she tied with a handkerchief. She would become an ailing elderly gentleman with arthritis in his arm and a toothache in the jaw. The handkerchief also hid the soft skin on her face. Not a single person would know she did not have a beard.

> A **poultice** was a warm mound of clay, meal, or other sticky substance. It was used as a medicine. It was warmed and applied to the skin to soothe aching joints and swelling. The poultice was held on with a sling or cloth.

William risked terrible danger by buying clothes for Ellen's disguise. It was against the law for white people to sell clothing or other items to slaves. But William knew there must be greedy people out there to take his hard-earned money. As a cabinetmaker, he was required to give most of his wages to his owner but was allowed to keep a small part for himself.

After several days of sneaking around to different stores, he had everything except pants. Ellen made clothes for her owners, so it was no problem to make a pair for herself. Hiding the clothes was easy. Her owner had trusted Ellen enough to give her a small room by herself and a dresser with a lock.

Their plan was nearly complete. All they needed were passes from their owners. Now they would have to lie with straight faces. Both asked for a few days off to visit each other. Lucky for them, it was Christmas season. Even the meanest slave owner often let people visit family around Christmastime.

Now that the time had come, Ellen was more frightened than ever. She cried when her husband cut off her hair. As she thought of what she must do over the next few days,

> Blacks were not free to travel without a **pass.** This permission slip was written and signed by the owner. Any slave could be stopped by a white man and required to show his pass. If he was without one, he could be punished or whipped on the spot. In some areas of the South, free blacks were also required to carry a pass from a white man who served as a guardian.

she was no longer sure she had the courage. But Ellen had a strong faith in God. After praying for his protection, she stopped her tears and was ready to go. She slipped into her disguise and became an official slave owner.

Once they started on their dangerous journey, they were nearly discovered. Because William had to travel with the slaves and Ellen with the slave owners, they could not talk when they ran into problems. On their first train out of Macon, Georgia,

The Crafts escaped from Macon, Georgia, on a train, and caught a steamship in Savannah. This is the Cotton Exchange of Savannah, once one of the busiest in the South.

William's heart jumped when he saw the gentleman he worked for outside his train car! The cabinetmaker stuck his head into the cars, but luckily did not see William in the corner with his back turned.

Ellen had an even more frightening experience. Mr. Cray, a longtime friend of her owner, sat down right next to her. As was the custom among Southern travelers, he started a friendly conversation. Ellen decided to pretend she was hard of hearing and ignored him. He soon found someone else to talk with. When he left the train at the next stop, Ellen was almost shaking with fear.

Over the next 4 days and nights, William and Ellen continued their charade as owner and slave. It meant using all the strength, acting skills, and courage they had to get them through their dangerous journey. This required them to board several trains and steamers. They had to hire carriages, buys meals, and rent hotel rooms.

While these skills were ordinary for any white man, the Crafts had no experience in such matters. Any small mistake on their part would make people suspicious. Discovery meant punishment and possibly death. Their path to freedom was long and complicated, crossing several states. They traveled through six major cities: Savannah, Georgia; Charleston, South Carolina; Wilmington, North Carolina; Richmond,

Carriages were an important means of transportation in Savannah. The Crafts traveled by ship, carriage, and train on their 1,000-mile journey to freedom.

Frank Leslie's Illustrated Newspaper

Virginia; Washington, D.C.; and on to Baltimore, Maryland. Freedom awaited them not far from there in Philadelphia, Pennsylvania.

On their journey, William was forced to sleep on top of cotton bales on ship decks instead of inside where it was dry and warm. On trains, he slept on top of baggage in the cars where the slaves rode. He spent his days waiting on his "owner"—polishing his boots, cutting up his food at meals, carrying his luggage, and preparing the poultices for his "arthritis." Along the journey, he bought a white beaver top hat to disguise himself. He also picked up tips from other blacks on how to escape, and who would help him in Philadelphia.

Poor Ellen was forced to endure conversation after conversation about lazy slaves, cotton prices, and evil abolitionists. How hard it was for her to keep quiet and not argue. On more than one occasion she received compliments on how attentive her male slave was. And she even got a few negative remarks from other white Southern planters that she was entirely too polite and was spoiling him.

> An **abolitionist** was a person dedicated to ending the practice of slavery. Many of them risked being fined or thrown in prison to hide runaways.

At a fine Charleston hotel everyone was convinced she was an important, wealthy planter. Ellen even had the nerve to leave tips for the servants. One of them pulled William aside to tell him that his owner was the most important guest who had been there in nearly a year. He is "a big bug," he said—which meant he was very important. Whenever Ellen ran into problems or thought she was going to be discovered, she pretended to feel sick and called her "slave" to take to her to rest.

As William and Ellen had expected, she was asked to sign at some stops on their journey. In Charleston at the Customs House, the officer in charge became very angry and mean when Ellen asked him to sign for her. She explained about her hand being crippled from arthritis. He stubbornly announced he would not sign for the elderly traveler. Fearing their journey was coming to an end, the pair was frozen with terror.

At that moment, a young military officer appeared at their side. Lucky for William and Ellen, he remembered them from the steamship trip from Savannah. This Southern gentleman, slightly drunk from too much brandy, proceeded to tell the Customs House officer that he knew the elderly gentleman and his family well. He said they were fine people. Of course, the Crafts were happy to pretend that this was a dear, longtime friend. In the days to come, the young officer would regret his friendly comments when he learned of the Crafts' escape.

At last, the owner and slave arrived in Baltimore, the last slave port and their last stop to reaching freedom in Philadelphia. William could feel the excitement

The Old Exchange and Custom House of Charleston, South Carolina. The Crafts were almost discovered here when Ellen was asked to sign a legal document. She could not read and write.

Library of Congress

growing as he put his owner into the train car and headed for the passenger car for blacks.

Imagine his terror when an officer grabbed him by the arm and began to question him. He told William he would not be going any further until his owner could prove ownership. Both were ordered to report to the office right away. They were sick with fright.

Having come so far, this was a terrible blow. Freedom was just a few hours away. Ellen was not about to give up now. She threw back her shoulders and tried to appear as important as she possibly could. She marched into the office and demanded that they be allowed to go. It soon became clear that no amount of acting on her part was going to persuade this officer. He wanted to know if they had relatives in the city or anyone who could testify to their good character. When they answered no, his decision was harsh. "We shan't let you go," he announced.

Philadelphia, Pennsylvania, was known as the City of Brotherly Love. Many people there worked to end slavery. Approximately 340,000 men from Pennsylvania signed up as Union soldiers. The longest and bloodiest battle of the war was fought in Pennsylvania at Gettysburg. There, President Lincoln gave his famous Gettysburg Address when he dedicated the battlefield as a national military cemetery for soldiers who fought there.

When the Crafts arrived in Philadelphia, Pennsylvania, on Christmas Day, they were on free soil at last.

As the train started to leave, the conductor from the last leg of the journey wandered into the office. He told the officer that the owner and slave had been on his train and caused him no problems. Maybe it was his words, the sympathy of the other passengers watching, or the fact that the old man was so ill, but the officer finally let them pass. With pounding hearts, they quickly boarded the train before he changed his mind.

The terrible strain of pretending for so long exhausted the Crafts. When the train rolled into Philadelphia, William says he "rejoiced and thanked God with all my heart and soul for his great kindness and tender mercy in watching over us and bringing us safely through."

As for Ellen, she became so weak she collapsed when they arrived at a safe boarding house. She had been brave for the past 1,000 miles, but then her strength left her. Their first day of freedom was on a Sunday and a special Sunday at that. It was Christmas Day. The weary travelers found the strength to get on their knees. William wrote: "We poured out our heartfelt gratitude to God, for his goodness in enabling us to overcome so many perilous difficulties, in escaping out of the jaws of the wicked."

The Crafts may have been safe for the moment, but their story did not end in Philadelphia. There were more adventures and close calls to come. The abolitionists of the community took the Crafts under their wings right away. Mr. Barkley Ivens and his wife were particularly kind to Ellen and William. They invited them to stay in their home while they recovered from their long, stressful journey.

When the Ivens family learned that the Crafts did not read and write, they started lessons for them immediately. At the end of their 3 weeks' stay, they had already learned to spell and write their own names. Next, they convinced William and Ellen they should keep moving north. Boston, they said, would be a safer place. Although slave owners legally could recapture blacks there, the abolitionists usually prevented this.

For nearly 2 years, William and Ellen lived in Boston working peacefully as cabinetmaker and seamstress. But their quiet lives were disrupted when they learned that 2 slave hunters, Mr. Hughes and Mr. Knight, were on their path. Dr. Collins, Ellen's owner, wanted her back. It had been only one month since the Fugitive Slave Law passed and he wasted no time.

William Lloyd Garrison was the editor of the newspaper *The Liberator*. He was the most hotheaded and well-known abolitionist in the country. He demanded an immediate end to slavery. When he first started writing for abolitionist publications, he was thrown in jail because of the way he wrote about slave traders. He kept up his written attacks of slavery from 1831 until 1865 when it was outlawed. He also worked for equal treatment of women in the Anti-Slavery Society.

But the local abolitionists acted quickly too. A new group called the League of Freedom was organized. Its purpose was to fight the new fugitive slave law. Together with help from the local paper, *The Liberator,* they asked people to be on the watch for slave hunters who were after the Crafts. Eagerly, they did. Three of the league's members took Ellen from home to home, keeping her safe.

William went with league president Lewis Hayden to his home on Beacon Hill. Hayden was ready to die to save William. He and his friends rounded up their guns and two kegs of gunpowder. They put out the word that they would blow up the house before they would ever surrender an innocent man.

On top of it all, the league members had Hughes and Knight arrested! But that did not last long. Soon they were out of jail, tracking down William and Ellen. The brave abolitionists decided a face-to-face showdown was necessary. They rounded up as many league members as they could find and went straight to the slave hunters' hotel. Here they told them in strong words that they were neither welcome in Boston nor safe. Then they offered to escort them to a train. The slave hunters tried to shrug off their threats, but some hours later Hughes and Knight nervously fled the city.

Dr. Collins was quite furious that his slave hunters were treated so shabbily in Boston. He wrote an angry letter to President Millard

William Lloyd Garrison

Library of Congress

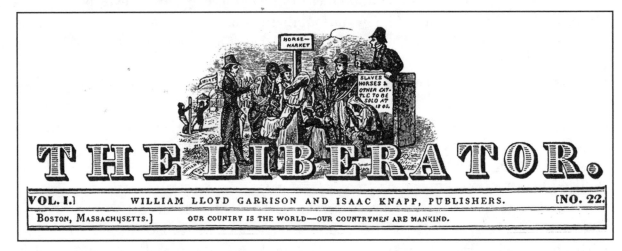

The masthead of William Lloyd Garrison's newspaper, **The Liberator.** ***Garrison assisted the Crafts with stories in his paper.***

Library of Congress

This is the cover of a magazine of the American Anti-Slavery Society. Their members protected runaway slaves. One abolitionist hid William Craft in his home and threatened to blow it up if the slave hunters came.

Library of Congress

Fillmore, who announced his plans to use Federal troops to arrest the Crafts. William and Ellen then realized they could never be safe in their own country. Their abolitionist friends made plans to send them overseas.

That was not as easy as it sounded. Every naval officer had his eyes peeled for a glimpse of the Crafts, who were now nationally famous. There was no way they could ever board a ship in Boston. Members of the League of Freedom arranged for them to travel overland to Portland, Maine, then Canada, and on to England.

Before they left the United States, they had one wish fulfilled. Although they knew their "jumping the broom" ceremony meant they were married in their hearts and in the eyes of God, William and Ellen wanted a legally recognized wedding. A well-known Massachusetts abolitionist, Rev. Theodore Parker, was happy to marry them. As wedding gifts, he gave them a Bible and a knife—to protect their souls and their freedom, he said.

The Crafts lived for 17 years in England. There, they raised their family of 5 children. They became quite well-educated people partly because of their friendship with Lady Noel Byron, the wife of Lord George Byron, the famous poet. Across England, they traveled, speaking against slavery. During their years there, William published his famous book and slave narrative, *Running a Thousand Miles for Freedom.*

President Millard Fillmore was ready to send troops to arrest William and Ellen Craft. Abolitionists hid them from slave hunters.

Library of Congress

After the Civil War ended, the Crafts returned to the United States. One of their dreams was to start a school to educate blacks. They did this for many years on their own farm in Georgia. But the Ku Klux Klan, a secret society that committed violence against blacks, burned down their first school. Eventually, the expense of running the school became too much and it failed. Tragically, the farm was auctioned off and the Crafts ended their lives in poverty.

The bravery of this young slave couple lives on in the hearts of those who read their daring story. They may have ended their lives penniless, but they were rich in spirit. Their names live on in Hammersmith, England, where Craft Court is named after them, and the local folk know their story well. In Georgia, Ellen received her long overdue recognition in 1996 when she was named a Georgia Woman of Achievement.

Ellen and William Craft crossed through several states disguised as a slave owner and slave.

Chapter 4

Slave Girl in the Attic
Harriet Ann Jacobs (1813-1897)

Linda's heart pounded in terror. She covered her ears to stop the noises of the angry search party. Lying on her back in the darkness, she could not stop her arms and legs from trembling. She could hear the men as they passed within inches of where she hid. "There will be five hundred lashes with the whip if I find out any of you are hiding her," yelled Dr. Flint, her owner.

The men tore through her grandmother's house in a frenzy, never thinking to check the attic space above the shed. Soon, they gathered their guns and dogs and continued through town. As they went, they posted signs that read: $100 reward for a runaway slave named Linda—an intelligent, bright mulatto girl, 21 years of age.

Once they left, quiet returned to the attic. It was so dark that Linda felt invisible. She could not tell whether it was day or night, but what did it matter? Either way, there was nothing for her to do but rest here on this hard wooden floor with the animal droppings. She jerked as another rat ran by and brushed against her leg.

Days and days of living in this prison had paralyzed her mind as well as her body. It was a struggle just to think. She felt her spirits sink into a deep, dark hole of despair. She longed for some fresh, cool air. The only air hole was an inch long. She pressed her face against it. All she got for her effort was hot, humid air that left her gasping for more. When she tried to turn over or to sit up, her head hit sharply against the attic roof and she nearly cried out. But she could never utter a sound for fear of being discovered. Dr. Flint's house was only 100 yards away.

$100 REWARD

Will be given for the apprehension and delivery of my Servant Girl HARRIET. She is a light mulatto, 21 years of age, about 5 feet 4 inches high, of a thick and corpulent habit, having on her head a thick covering of black hair that curls naturally, but which can be easily combed straight. She speaks easily and fluently, and has an agreeable carriage and address. Being a good seamstress, she has been accustomed to dress well, has a variety of very fine clothes, made in the prevailing fashion, and will probably appear, if abroad, tricked out in gay and fashionable finery. As this girl absconded from the plantation of my son without any known cause or provocation, it is probable she designs to transport herself to the North.

The above reward, with all reasonable charges, will be given for apprehending her, or securing her in any prison or jail within the U. States.

All persons are hereby forewarned against harboring or entertaining her, or bring in any way instrumental in her escape, under the most rigorous penalties of the law.

JAMES NORCOM

Edenton, N.C. June 30

From the American Beacon, *Norfolk, Virginia, July 4, 1835*

Reproduction of original newspaper advertisement (rendering by the author)

Down below, she could hear the laughter of Ben and Ellen, her 2 young children. How she longed to leave this dirty place and hold them in her arms. The tears ran down her face because she knew she could not. They were so young they might tell someone where she hid. Then she remembered Dr. Flint had threatened to kill her and that was why she was here. She wiped her face dry. Somehow she would find the courage to survive and escape.

As uncomfortable as she was, Linda chose to hide in this attic. Here she was free from her miserable life as a slave. Dr. Flint, her owner, could mistreat her no more. Although she was safe for the moment, she never dreamed it would be nearly seven years before she left her dark hiding place.

Who was this young slave girl? She called herself Linda and somehow she survived 27 years of enslavement in the South to tell the world her story. She did not use her own name when she wrote it to protect her family.

> In 1861, *Incidents in the Life of a Slave Girl* was published in Boston. It is a **slave narrative.** A narrative is the telling of a story. Many slaves told their life stories aloud, and friends recorded their words on paper.
>
> Linda's story is very important in the history of slavery. There are not many narratives of women slaves. This one tells about the mistreatment of a female slave by her owner.

Young Linda's story begins in the home of her parents. Her early years were happy ones. Her father was a talented carpenter whose owner let him work for himself. Linda's parents were light-skinned slaves, known as mulattos, who lived together in a cabin. This was unusual for most shared living quarters with several families.

> **Mulatto**—The word slave owners used to describe a person with one white parent and one black parent.

Linda's grandmother was an important person in her life. Around town, she was called Aunt Marthy, a very smart, hard-working woman. Known as an excellent cook, she sold her delicious crackers to buy clothes and extra food for the family. Someday, she hoped to buy her children's freedom.

When Linda was 6, her mother died. She went to live with her mother's owner, a woman who taught her to read, write, and spell, even though it was against the law. She remembers these years as a happy time:

> I would sit by her side for hours, sewing diligently, with a heart as free from care as that of any free-born white child. When she thought I was tired, she would send me out to run and jump; and away I bounded, to gather berries or flowers to decorate her room.

Both her father and her owner died when Linda was 12. Hoping her kind mistress had arranged for her freedom, Linda was instead given to a 3-year-old niece,

Linda's grandmother worked hard just like the women in this photograph. She baked delicious crackers in her spare time. She sold them and bought extra food and clothes for her grandchildren.

Library of Congress

the child of Dr. and Mrs. Flint. Her happy days ended. She discovered that her new owners were nothing like her old one.

Dr. Flint immediately put Linda's grandmother up for sale even though he knew she was promised her freedom. Fortunately, a sympathetic relative bought Marthy and set her free. Mrs. Flint was no better with her bad temper. She became most upset when her Sunday dinner was not on the table on time. When the food was dished up, she went by each cooking pot and spit into it. This way no one could have any of the leftovers.

Her husband, who loved to eat, whipped the cook if he did not like the food. Sometimes he made her eat all the food as a punishment. When he was really angry, he locked her up for a day and a night even though she had a young baby to feed. Linda also saw the doctor beat a man until the blood poured from his back.

Although she was unhappy, Linda settled into her new life. She found that the rustic church in the woods was very important to her people. There they were happy when shouting and singing. They often made up the words to their own hymns: "Ole Satan's church is here below. Up to God's free church I hope to go." Many married and baptized their children even though it was not legal.

Every year a muster, or military drill, was held. The white men would gather together their horses, dogs, and weapons to remind the black people who was in charge. One year, the muster turned nasty. A Virginia slave had escaped and killed many white people. Slave owners in Linda's community were in a state of terror. They ransacked the slaves' cabins, stole their belongings, and whipped many innocent people. They destroyed the little church in

Nat Turner was a Virginia slave. In 1831, he and 60 other slaves killed 60 white people. Nat's owner and family were among those murdered. Virginia military troops captured and hung Nat and 20 other slaves. Close to 100 innocent blacks were killed during this time.

the woods and made the slaves attend the white services. The violence went on for weeks until the slave was captured.

There were times like Christmas, when people were happy. Linda said, "Even slave mothers try to gladden the hearts of their little ones on that occasion." Her

Nat Turner is captured in this drawing. He was the Virginia slave who murdered his owner's family. Linda remembered that many innocent slaves were punished before Nat was captured. The little church in the woods where her family worshipped was destroyed during this time.

Harper's Weekly

grandmother made new clothes and toys, and stockings were filled. Men in the families caught a turkey or a pig—without asking their owners—and everyone feasted.

To the children, the most exciting part was getting up early to see the Johnkannaus. Two men dressed up like a cow. Others played triangles, jawbones, or a hand-made drum called the gumbo box. Singing and dancing,

> The **Johnkannaus** was a troop of male slaves that provided Christmas entertainment when Linda was a young girl.

these men knocked on every door of the neighboring plantations begging pennies and rum. Even the slave owners donated. But the happiness of Christmas quickly faded. Every year on the first of January, many slaves were auctioned or hired out. Bitter tears fell as families were split up, never to meet again.

When Linda turned 14, she was very pretty and Dr. Flint noticed. He began to follow her during her work. Her life became a nightmare. Everywhere she went he was there whether she was taking a walk or visiting her parents' grave.

It soon became clear to Linda that Dr. Flint found her very attractive. This was very upsetting and terrifying for her. She was in love with a black man and wanted a husband and family of her own. But this was not to be. Slave owners did not encourage slaves to marry.

Dr. Flint told Linda he was building a special cabin for her where he wanted them to meet, away from everyone. She was quite bold and told him no. He begged and promised her the life of a fine lady with excellent food and better clothes.

When that did not work, he tried to frighten her. Every hour of the day she dreaded seeing him because he screamed, threatened, or cursed at her. He told her he would whip her or kill her if she did not obey him.

By now, Mrs. Flint knew what was going on and turned vicious with jealousy. Linda tried everything she knew to stop Dr. Flint but she had no power. She was just a slave with no rights under the law.

Soon, she knew she would have to do something. The cabin was being built, and in months it would be finished. She decided that although Dr. Flint owned her, he could never control her mind or her feelings. She decided to choose another man for whom she had some respect. Maybe then the doctor would leave her alone. Mr. Sands was a kind, unmarried white man who was sympathetic to her problems. They started seeing a lot of one another. Many months later her son Ben was born. They also had a daughter named Ellen.

Linda thought of going to her grandmother for help. When Dr. Flint heard this, Linda said: **"He threatened me with death, and worse than death if I made any complaint."**

When Dr. Flint heard this news, he flew into a jealous rage. Mr. Sands wanted to buy Linda and her children, but the doctor would not hear of it. Instead, he sent her to the plantation to work. Before this, she was assigned housework and he never allowed anyone to whip her. She heard he had plans to take her children from her grandmother's home and bring them to the plantation too. She could never let that happen. Once on the plantation, they might be sold.

Linda knew it was time to run away. She packed her few belongings and began her life as a fugitive. For the next 17 years, she would flee and hide from Dr. Flint and his family.

The day following Linda's escape, her grandmother's home was searched as were all the ships leaving the docks. Teams were sent out that night and a $100 reward was promised. Linda first hid at the home of a friend and then in the woods where she became deathly ill from a snakebite. Then she lived in the closet of a white woman who was her grandmother's friend. The search parties were always at work so she could not escape. The vicious Dr. Flint put her aunt, brother, and two children in jail until someone confessed where Linda was hiding.

This woman was punished for running away. Linda knew this could happen to her so she hid for 7 years until she was sure she could safely escape to the North.

Dr. Flint then followed a rumor and made a trip to New York looking for Linda. He returned home short of money and sold Linda's brother and children to the next slave trader. It was lucky for them that Mr. Sands secretly arranged to buy them back. When Dr. Flint heard what happened, he was furious. He had more members of Linda's family arrested.

It was becoming more and more dangerous for Linda to remain in the same spot. A new hiding place had to be found, and her family began to search. When the time came to move, she disguised herself in sailor clothes and walked through town to her grandmother's house.

When Linda crawled into her new "home" she had no idea that she would be there for 7 years. Her Uncle Phillip made a place for her under the roof of a small shed attached to her grandmother's house. This attic space, full of mice and red ants, was only nine by seven feet and only three feet high. It was cold in the winter and hot in the summer. She had one tiny air hole so she could see into the street and read and sew. Her relatives fed her at night.

To add to her torment, she could hear her children playing outside. They were too young to be told where she was, so Linda had to listen only.

In winter, the rain leaked in and she became very sick. For awhile she lost the ability to speak and was losing the use of her arms and legs.

To throw Dr. Flint off track, Aunt Marthy invited the town constable for Christmas dinner just to prove that

> Linda spent 7 miserable years hiding in an attic loft. Yet she said, "**I would have chosen this, rather than my lot as a slave.**"

this was not Linda's hiding place. Linda then wrote a letter to Dr. Flint saying she was living in the North. A friend put this letter on a ship headed north and had

For 7 years, Linda lived in the attic of a shed like this one. It was attached to her grandmother's home. She was afraid of her owner, who threatened her and her children.

Library of Congress

someone mail it from there. This led Dr. Flint to visit New York 2 more times trying to find her.

For 6 years and 11 months, Linda suffered in misery in the attic loft. Both her mental and physical health were near ruin. Her grandmother was getting older and the stress of hiding her was a terrible strain. In addition, Mr. Sands married and sent Ellen north to work for his new relatives. Linda worried about what kind of life Ellen would have. She wanted to go to the free states to be with her daughter.

Linda's friend Peter had been searching for a long time for a safe way for her to escape. Finally, he found a ship captain that he felt he could pay and trust. She safely sailed north to freedom in New York.

Fortunately for Linda, the next family she worked for, the Bruces, were abolitionists. Abolitionists were people working to stop or to abolish slavery. She was treated very kindly during her work there as nurse to their children. The Fugitive Slave Law of 1850 made it a crime to hide a slave. Anyone doing so risked a $1,000 fine or a 6-months' prison term. The Bruce family gladly hired her in spite of the danger to themselves.

Linda could not relax yet. The stubborn Dr. Flint made searching for Linda his lifelong goal and continued to stay on her trail. Somehow she always received word that he was coming and left. During her life in the North, she fled from him 5 times. She lived for brief periods in Boston, the New England states, and London. The friends who hid her convinced Linda to write her story of slavery. In her spare time, she began to do that.

> When Linda heard she was free, she said: **"When I rode home in the cars, I was no longer afraid to unveil my face and look at people as they passed...My heart was exceedingly full. I remembered how my poor father...tried to buy me as a small child...I hoped his spirit was rejoicing over me now."**

In 1852, Linda received word that Dr. Flint died. His daughter and son-in-law traveled to the North to claim her as their property. Again, she had to run away. The Bruce family convinced Flint's relatives to sell Linda to them or they would help her escape to England. They finally agreed and at last she was free of the curse of the Flints.

Now that Linda was free, she wanted to finish her story. A friend helped her with the writing. She was Maria Child, the newspaper editor of the *National Anti-Slavery Standard*. Many people did not believe Linda's story when it was published—even though it was signed and witnessed by a neighbor

> **"I know that it is full of living truths. I have been well acquainted with the author since boyhood. I know of her treatment and...of her seven years' concealment. I am now a resident of Boston, and am a living witness to the truth."**—George W. Lowther

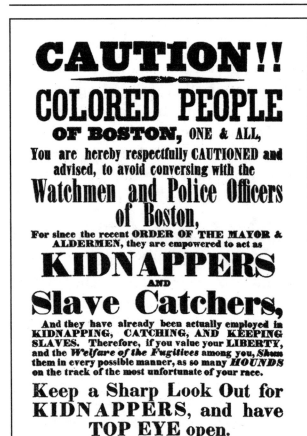

When Linda lived in the North, she often saw advertisements like this. She had to be very careful to whom she talked. Under the Fugitive Slave Act, she could be captured and returned to Dr. Flint.

Library of Congress

who knew her story was true. People thought that Maria Child made it up or exaggerated to help the abolitionists.

Another problem was that Linda Brent was not her real name. She chose to use this name as a secret identity because she wanted to protect the people who helped her escape. Also, she wished to protect her children and Mr. Sands from any scandal.

During the Civil War, Linda worked as a teacher and as a nurse for black troops in Washington, D.C. She also helped escaped slaves who crossed the Union lines, and ones who were captured during battle. Her book was a valuable weapon for the abolitionists as an example of slavery. Hers was a firsthand account of mistreatment of female slaves. A year after her book came out, it was published in England under the title *The Deeper Wrong*.

Linda died at the age of 84 in 1897. In the years following her death, her book was ignored. People would not accept it because no one knew who she really was or where these events took place. Soon, her important story was forgotten. None of the characters are alive today to tell their story.

This much we know. In the 1980s, scholars at Harvard University were able to identify the true author. They did this from letters written to Maria Child and the family that Linda lived with in Boston. They were able to identify Linda's owner, the main characters, and the town where the story took place. The newspaper ad placed by the doctor when she ran away was found too. Also, her brother in England had written his life story for the newspapers the same year her book was published. Being an ocean apart, it was hard to believe they could have made up the same account.

As for the true identity of Linda Brent, one must travel to a small North Carolina town to uncover her secrets. There in Edenton you can learn about this courageous woman and writer as well as the town where she lived. Her real name was Harriet Ann Jacobs.

These slaves were left behind by their owner. They became contrabands, or captives turned soldiers. Linda assisted people like these.

During the Civil War, Linda helped runaways and served as a nurse for wounded soldiers and contrabands. Contrabands were the enslaved who ran away during the war and crossed over the Union lines. Some ran across the lines themselves and others were captured and put to work for the army.

The man who owned Harriet was a physician who was active in his church and community. His name was Dr. James Norcom. Samuel Tredwell Sawyer, a U.S. congressman of the Whig Party, was Mr. Sands. The white woman who hid Harriet was named Martha Hoskins Rombough Blount. Her house is gone now, replaced by a gas station. Aunt Marthy, who hid her granddaughter for all those years, was really Molly Horniblow. And a parking lot is all that remains of the attic prison where rats and mice once scurried across the feet of a brave, young slave girl.

> On May 18, 1998, a North Carolina highway historical marker was erected in Edenton, North Carolina. It honors **Harriet Ann Jacobs**—the true author of *Incidents in the Life of a Slave Girl.*
>
> In 1997, Jacobs was inducted into the North Carolina Literary Hall of Fame.

A painting of Harriet Ann Jacobs at age 81

North Carolina Division of Archives and History

This photo is thought to be of Dr. James Norcom, owner of Harriet Jacobs.

North Carolina Division of Archives and History

Chapter 5

Freedom or Family
Henry Bibb (1815–1854)

The blood-curdling sound pierced the peacefulness of the dark and quiet night, and Henry woke with a pounding fear in his heart. There was no mistaking this terrible noise—a pack of wolves was howling in hunger. They were so close he could hear them approaching. Their eyes glowed and lit up the blackness as they slowly crept forward.

Henry's daughter, Mary Frances, was just a baby. The dreadful sounds of the wild animals alarmed her and she cried hysterically. Nothing would comfort her. Her mother, Malinda, was shaking. She could not bear the thought of dying out here in these woods. In her imagination, she pictured wolves tearing her flesh and eating her baby girl.

In that terrible moment when he was sure he would die, Henry thought about his life and what had brought him here. All the humiliating and painful parts of being enslaved flashed through his mind: the whippings and chains, the hunger, and never being able to protect his family. He wondered about heaven. Would his owner, Deacon Whitfield, be there? If so, it must not be a kind and loving place as he had always imagined.

The reason he was out in the woods to begin with was because he only wanted to attend a

Wolves threatened Henry and his family.

Library of Congress

Henry Bibb wanted to go to a prayer meeting, but his owner said no. He went anyway and received a beating that nearly killed him.

Harper's Monthly

prayer meeting. Even though Mr. Whitfield was a church deacon, he forbade Henry to go. Henry had always been bold, so he decided to sneak off anyway. When he returned, Malinda was terror-stricken. Deacon Whitfield had threatened to give Henry 500 lashes the next day—a whipping that could easily kill him.

Upon hearing this news, Henry decided to run. He only made matters worse by stealing a mule to get away. The penalty for theft was death. It was not long before he could hear bloodhounds on his trail, and the mule was causing problems. He could not stop it from braying and giving away his location.

Henry circled back to the farm and left the mule. Malinda told him the deacon was planning to sell him after he gave him the beating of his life. With that news, the family decided to escape together on foot.

They headed for the Red River swamps and lived on parched corn, paw-paws, and wild berries for a week. Weak with hunger, they hoped to cross the river but could not find a safe spot. Finally, Henry grasped his baby in his arms and took to the river, thinking, "If we perish let us all perish together in this stream."

Any joy they felt in making it to the other side quickly disappeared. They were on an island. Exhausted and discouraged, they slept on beds of leaves. They had only been asleep a short while, when the wolves began their frightful wailing.

During the years 1850–1859, nearly **1,000 enslaved people** ran away every year. Eighty percent of them were males aged 16–35. Often they were running to escape a punishment, or repeated cruelty, from their owners and overseers.

Henry knew he had to do something. If he just sat there, the wolves would attack. He thought if he must die, he would "die striving to protect my little family from destruction, die striving to escape from slavery." The only weapon he had was a big knife he stole from the deacon. Malinda grabbed Mary Frances and a big piece of wood to defend them.

With courage in his heart and a blade in hand, Henry charged straight at the pack of bloodthirsty wolves. His fear made him brave and strong, and he let forth the most frightening screams his lungs could possibly make. The wolves were startled by such loud, ferocious behavior and ran for the woods.

In later years, Henry said:

> I often look back to that dangerous event...and wonder how I could have run such a risk....to leave home and friends and go to the wild forest and lay out on the cold ground night after night without covering, and live on parched corn? What would induce me to take my family and go into the swamps...among the snakes and alligators with all the liabilities of being destroyed by them, hunted down with bloodhounds, or lay myself liable to be shot down like the wild beasts of the forest? Nothing I say, nothing but the strongest love of liberty, humanity, and justice to myself and family.

Whipping was a common form of punishment by slave owners. It was also called flogging. Some owners sent their slaves to workhouses to be whipped. Many blacks had scars the rest of their lives from the severe whippings they received.

Library of Congress

Henry was soon to pay for his quest for freedom. His family finally made their way off the island, and they wandered through the woods for days. They knew their luck was running out when they heard the sounds of bloodhounds in the distance. When the slave hunters finally closed in, Henry surrendered in hopes of making the punishment less for his family.

The next morning, Henry was stripped of his clothing, and his arms and legs were staked to the ground. The overseer gave him lash after lash until his back was a bloody mess of raw flesh. When he was finished, Deacon Whitfield added a few more lashes himself and ordered 8 licks with a wooden paddle that was known to raise blisters. To finish off his punishment, salt water was poured over his wounds. For many days, he was too sick to work.

After that, Henry was not allowed to sleep in the cabin with his family. He was placed in chains away from everyone else. A heavy iron collar was made to go around his neck. It had prongs above his head that held a bell, making it impossible for him to sleep. If he decided to run again, the bell would give him away. Deacon Whitfield also threatened Henry, warning him that "No negro should ever get away from him alive."

This frightening story of escape and punishment is one of many in the life of Henry Bibb. From the time of his birth on May 10, 1815, on a Kentucky plantation, Henry seemed born to run. Run he did—a total of 7 times from 7 owners. He also risked his life again and again by returning home to rescue his family.

Henry's first owner was David White. His mother, Mildred Jackson, was a slave and some historians think that Kentucky Senator James Bibb may have been Henry's

After his escape, Henry was chained and not allowed to be with his family.

Library of Congress

This man is modeling an iron collar that was used to chain up runaway slaves. Some slave owners hung bells on the collars so they would know where the slaves were at all times. Henry Bibb had to wear an iron collar after running away.

Library of Congress

father. The young daughter of his owner was Henry's childhood playmate. But their friendship ended with bitter cruelty when young Henry was hired out to work at other plantations. Mr. White used all of the money that Henry earned to pay for school for his daughter.

So Henry decided early in life that he wanted his freedom. He felt in his heart that God had made men to be free, and he was willing to take the risk and the punishment if necessary to get that freedom. When he was first flogged at the farm of Mr. and Mrs. Vires in 1835, he made his first escape. Even though he was caught, Henry ran again. The Vires gave up and sent him home to Mr. White.

Henry now had a taste of freedom. When his mistress beat him, Henry just disappeared. One trick he learned was to carry a horse's bridle with him. If a white man stopped to question him, he would say his owner sent him after a runaway mare.

To protect himself, Henry even visited a conjurer. He paid an old man to mix a special potion of alum and salt that was supposed to create a spell against whippings. But it did not work—Henry got one anyway.

Another conjurer told him to sprinkle a mixture of dried manure, red pepper, and white people's hair in his owner's bedroom. This set him to sneezing so much that Henry decided to stop for fear of being caught.

When Henry got old enough to be interested in girls, he tried some spells on them too. The conjurer told him to scratch the skin of the girl he loved with a frog bone. When he did this, she was furious. It hurt. Next, he needed the hair of a girl to make a magic potion. When he yanked a hair from her head, of course she screamed in pain. Henry decided to give up on spells. They were not helping his love life.

> A **conjurer** is a person who makes magic spells. In his story of slavery, Henry wrote about superstitions. Some blacks believed in witchcraft and passed on their beliefs and skills for making potions to the younger slaves.

When he met Malinda, Henry did not need any spells. This beautiful, young woman lived on the farm of Mr. William Gatewood 4 miles away. Malinda was known for her beauty, singing talent, and kindness. He could tell she loved him when he looked into her shining eyes. After a year's engagement, they were married in a slave ceremony.

Henry thought he was lucky when he was sold to Mr. Gatewood. Now he and Malinda could be on the same plantation. But he had not thought it all through. Every time Malinda was whipped or punished or abused, there was nothing he could do. He said, "It was more than I could bear."

The couple soon became parents to a baby girl. Mary Frances was such a joy to them. One day when her mother was working in the fields, Mary Frances had to stay behind with the mistress. When her mother returned, the baby girl's face was covered in bruises. Henry and Malinda were sickened over this cruel treatment, but they had no rights to defend their children. Black people could not testify against whites in court.

After three years of marriage, Henry made a decision. He was going to escape to Canada. He could no longer bear seeing his family in such misery. He said:

> The voice of liberty was thundering in my very soul, "Be free, oh Man! be free." I had counted the cost and was fully prepared to make the sacrifice. I

must forsake friends and neighbors, wife and child, or consent to live and die a slave.

During the Christmas holidays, Henry told his owner he was going to work for extra money. Instead, he crossed the Ohio River into the free state of Indiana. That night he boarded a steamship for Cincinnati, Ohio. He did not sleep a wink for fear of being discovered. Once there, he met some abolitionists. Henry did not know such people existed. With their directions in his head and his eyes on the North Star at night, he set out to find Canada.

Finding enough food and places to sleep was more difficult than he realized. When he found a settlement of free blacks in Perrysburgh, Ohio, he decided to spend the winter earning money. His plan was to return to Kentucky to rescue Malinda and Mary Frances and take them to Canada too. He even bought a pair of fake whiskers so slave hunters would not recognize him.

> There were 500,000 **free blacks** in 1860. Half of these lived in the slave states. One-third of the free black population dwelled in large towns or cities. In New Orleans, there were 10,000 free blacks. In 1850, there were 3,441 free black people living in Charleston, South Carolina. Many were professionals or skilled artisans. Some of them even owned slaves.

Henry's family was overjoyed to see him again. They decided that Malinda would leave on a Saturday night, one week after Henry, and buy herself a ticket to Cincinnati. They would meet there on Sunday.

Back in Ohio, Henry was double-crossed. Two men pretending to be abolitionists were really slave hunters. They were after the $300 reward for Henry. One afternoon while Henry was digging a cellar to earn money, the hunters cornered him. Henry ran for the fence but was caught going over it. He said:

> I kicked and struggled with all my might to get away but without success. I kicked a new cloth coat off of his back while he was holding onto my leg. I kicked another in his eye...By this time, there was a crowd with clubs to beat me back. Finally they succeeded in dragging me from the fence and overpowered me....and choked me almost to death.

Henry spent that night in jail waiting for the journey back home. On board a boat the next day, Henry thought about jumping in the river and ending his life. The hunters told him that two black men in Cincinnati had turned him in for the money. The hunters tried to get Henry to come to work for them. They promised to make him rich, but Henry could never agree to that.

As the boat floated farther south, Henry realized he was not going home. These slave hunters planned to sell him. He would never see his little family again. When they arrived in Louisville, Kentucky, the men found a hotel. Three of them slept in Henry's room to keep him from escaping.

The next day, the men went to find someone to buy Henry. They left him with Dan Lane, a mean slave hunter with a nasty reputation. Fortunately for Henry, Lane got sick and had to go to the horse stable. With guns and bowie knives for protection, he dragged Henry along. While getting sick in the back end of the horse stall, Lane turned his eyes for one instant. It only took Henry a split second to make a decision. He remembered:

> I nerved myself with all the moral courage I could command and bolted for the door...Dan was left in the stable to make ready for the race, or jump out into the street half dressed, and thereby disgrace himself before the public eye.

Dan Lane yelled for help, and it seemed to Henry like half the town was chasing after him. He had never run so fast in his life. He rounded every corner with lightning speed, dodging everything in his path.

Henry spotted a high fence and leaped over it only to land in a henhouse. This set off a bunch of squawking hens and barking, angry dogs. He headed for the streets again, charging wildly around more corners. At last, he ducked under a pile of lumber and hid there for almost 12 hours.

Once night fell, Henry mustered courage to wander out. By following the sounds of a bellowing cow, he found his way out of the dark city. The first place he headed was home for a brief visit with Malinda. How heartbreaking it was to leave her again, but he knew it was not safe for him to stay.

Malinda planned once more to meet him in Ohio. During this time, he heard the same slave traders were hunting him. He headed further north and waited nearly 8 months for Malinda. Finally, he knew he must go back for his family.

This time, Henry went to his mother's home to avoid discovery, but a young girl saw him. Because she talked, he was captured in a barn just a few mornings later. An angry group of men put him in irons and threw him in jail. Mr. Gatewood was more than tired of Henry's escapes. He marched Henry and his family to Louisville to be sold at the slave market.

Life in the jail was miserable with bedbugs, mosquitoes, and food which they were barely able to eat. This was nothing compared to the misery they experienced when they were next sold to Madison Garrison, a mean slave trader. He took the whole family to a workhouse where he kept them for several months. He was collecting as many slaves as he could to sell in New Orleans. During this time, he treated Malinda very cruelly and tried to attack her. There was nothing Henry could do to protect her.

Finally, the family was sold to Francis Whitfield, a respected Baptist deacon. The weary couple thought they had surely found a safe place and a kind owner. But they soon discovered that Whitfield had a mean streak. Henry said, "He was far more like what the people call the devil, than he was a deacon." His overseer was just as mean. He was under orders to get the slaves up at 4 a.m. and give them daily beatings before work. Everyone was poorly clothed and allowed to eat only once a day. The young women were treated worst of all.

As blacks labor in the field, Montgomery, Alabama can be seen in the background. This city was the first capital of the Confederacy. Later it was moved to Richmond, Virginia.

Frank Leslie's *Our Soldier in the Civil War*

Malinda was exhausted and sick while she lived on the Whitfield cotton plantation. She even lost their second baby. With a broken heart, Henry dug the baby's grave himself. The deacon never offered their child a decent burial or a coffin.

Not long after this, Henry and another man named old Jack ran away together. Unfortunately, they were discovered in a few days because Deacon Whitfield had posted signs everywhere about a $50 reward. Of course, both men were punished.

After so many escapes and so many whippings, most men would have stopped

> Henry and his family labored on a cotton plantation. The work of the slaves made many white men wealthy. **Farmland in the South in 1860 was valued at $1,871,000,000.** At that time, the South produced close to 4 million bales of cotton. By 1865, it was nearly half that amount. When the slaves in the District of Columbia were set free, the former slave owners were given $1,000,000 to make up for the money they lost.

running and accepted their fate—not Henry. It was at this point in his life that Henry went to the prayer meeting and stole the mule. Then, they had the frightening episode with the wolves and Henry received his near deadly beating.

Henry was still under punishment for running away when visitors arrived one sunny afternoon. A group of gamblers riding through Whitfield's plantation noticed

Henry Bibb worked on a cotton plantation owned by Deacon Francis Whitfield of Tennessee. The working conditions were so terrible that his wife, Malinda, stayed sick. She lost their second baby because her health was so poor. Henry buried the baby without a coffin.

In the South, cotton was king. Here workers are unloading bales of cotton. Like many blacks, Henry and his family picked cotton. The labor of blacks made many white men wealthy.

Henry's bell and chains. Deacon Whitfield was more than happy to get this trouble-maker off his hands when they asked whether Henry was for sale. Henry begged to go tell his family goodbye, but the deacon refused. In that quick instant, he was separated from his wife and child.

Henry's life changed after that. His new owners expected him to work, but they would have none of the cruelties of his old owner. They took off his chains, got him some decent clothes, and even gave him money and plenty of food. But Henry hardly noticed. All he wanted was to be with Malinda and Mary Frances.

When the gamblers were traveling near his old plantation again, Henry begged them to stop. They agreed to try and purchase his family. But Deacon Whitfield refused, saying he would never do anything that might bring Henry happiness. When Malinda and Mary Frances came into the yard to see Henry, Whitfield took the whip to them. The gamblers argued and pleaded, but it did no good. As they departed, Whitfield was still beating Henry's family while they cried for mercy. That December day in 1840 was the last time he saw them.

The gamblers may have been slave owners, but they felt a lot of sympathy for Henry. They were shocked at the cruelty they had seen. So they made a deal. If Henry could find someone to buy him, they would give him part of the money and tell him how to get to Canada.

As the gamblers rode through Arkansas and the Cherokee Indian Territory, they met a well-to-do Cherokee looking for a house servant. This sounded like the perfect place for Henry, so the gamblers made the sale. True to their word, they gave him some money and directions to the North.

Life with the Cherokees was quite different. This new owner did not have an overseer. Henry had plenty to eat and could go to church. Family members were not separated or sold away. Henry said this man "was the most reasonable and humane slaveholder" he belonged to.

The new owner was in very poor health when he bought Henry. Henry, however, stayed with him and did everything he asked. When the man died, he saw his chance for freedom. He helped prepare his body for burial, and then took off into the night. He crossed through the Indian territory by stealing a horse and finding friendly Indians to feed him.

Henry finally gained his freedom and became famous as an anti-slavery speaker in Michigan. But he never forgot his little family down South. In 1845, he tried one more time to rescue them. What he discovered broke his heart. Malinda sent word that she did not wish to see him. The day he left Whitfield plantation, she feared she would never see him again. So as years went by, she made a decision to start a new life. She was now the companion of a new owner and was comfortable if not happy.

With that sad news, Henry returned North a defeated man. He did marry again to schoolteacher Mary Miles, and wrote *Narrative of the Life and Adventures of Henry Bibb, An American Slave* in 1849. They moved to Sandwich, in Ontario, Canada, started a community for free blacks, and assisted the Underground Railroad. Henry even published *The Voice of the Fugitive,* the first African-American newspaper in Canada.

At this time, there was much discussion about what was best for the black community. Some like Frederick Douglass felt blacks should stay in the United States and fight for their rights. Another black leader, Martin Delany, believed strongly in a return to Africa movement. But Henry urged all enslaved people to come to freedom in Canada.

> By the time the Civil War started, nearly **14,000 black people** emigrated from the United States to Liberia, Africa. Some black leaders felt this was the best home for their people. Henry Bibb did not agree.

These children were freed blacks. Henry risked his life again and again to free his daughter, Mary Frances, and his wife, Malinda. He never succeeded.

Library of Congress

Henry Bibb was just 39 years old when he died, but he was a leader among his people. Though he risked his life many times, he was never able to free his beloved Malinda and Mary Frances. Before his death, he did live to see his mother and brothers come to Canada. Though Henry Bibb escaped and found fame, the one thing he truly wanted was beyond his reach—the freedom of his family.

Henry Bibb's story had so much cruelty and so many escapes that many people doubted it. A committee was appointed by the Detroit Liberty Association to determine the truth. They wrote to Henry's former owners and received letters back from the Gatewoods, Daniel Lane, a lawyer in Cincinnati, and a jailer in Louisville. In April of 1845, the group ruled that the story was real.

NARRATIVE

OF THE

LIFE AND ADVENTURES

OF

HENRY BIBB,

AN AMERICAN SLAVE,

WRITTEN BY HIMSELF.

WITH

AN INTRODUCTION

BY LUCIUS C. MATLACK.

~~~~~~~~~~~~~~~~~~

NEW YORK:
PUBLISHED BY THE AUTHOR; 5 SPRUCE STREET.
1849.

Title page from Henry Bibb's book, **Narrative of the Life and Adventures of Henry Bibb, An American Slave**
Courtesy of East Carolina University

An engraving of Henry Bibb from an original copy of his book. He escaped from slavery 7 times, but was never able to free his family.
Courtesy of East Carolina University

Chapter 6

The Most Famous Black Man in America
Booker T. Washington (1856–1915)

Booker was alone and he was scared. It was dark now and the woods around him seemed to be closing in. He hated being out there by himself. Behind every tree, he imagined someone waiting for him. The branches looked as if they had arms and fingers that were slowly growing in his direction. Maybe it was his imagination, but he thought he saw eyes staring at him.

He had heard stories about men hiding in these woods. People said if the deserters caught little slave boys, they would cut off their ears. He put his fingers around his ears as he thought about this.

A **deserter** was a soldier who ran away from the army. In the years 1863–65, an average of 1,250 men deserted from the Union army each week. A reward of $30 was offered for return of deserters.

Suddenly behind him, there was a crackle and a snap. His heart felt as if it had jumped into his throat and he started to run. Then he saw a small squirrel run by him in the moonlight. As his heartbeat slowly returned to normal, Booker continued down the road on his horse.

Why, he wondered, did he get this chore every week? It was a lot to ask of a 6-year-old boy. Ever since his owner died last year, Booker and his brother John were given harder and harder jobs to do. This was the one he dreaded the most: taking the corn to the mill to be ground and bringing it back home.

That bag of corn caused him problems every time. When he started out, someone at the plantation would throw the corn over the back of the horse. But it never stayed

After his owner died, Booker and his brother were expected to do more work. The job that he dreaded was taking the corn to the mill to be ground.

Library of Congress

on there long enough for him to get to the mill. The motion of the horse would jiggle the bag and soon one side of the bag would be heavier than the other one. Before long, it slid off and Booker tumbled down with it. Being such a small boy, he could not lift it high enough to get it back on the horse.

So he had to sit and wait for someone to come along and lift the bag. Sometimes it would be hours before anyone showed. On these days, Booker sat and cried. He knew what would happen if he arrived home late. The yelling was not so bad, but he hated the whipping he knew he would get.

Once again, it was nearly dark when he finally left the mill. It was only 3 miles home but it seemed more like 10. Booker swallowed hard and tried to ignore the frightening sounds of the forest. But nothing he could do made that terrible feeling in the pit of his stomach go away. The young slave boy just had to live with it. He and his horse slowly plodded for home.

Booker spent his early years living in a cabin that was the kitchen to a 207-acre Virginia farm. His shack was scorching hot in the summer, and bitter cold wind blew through the cracks in the winter. Booker's mother, Jane, was the cook. She worked over a blazing fire morning, noon, and evening to prepare food for the 20 people she fed every day. As for Booker's father, he never knew who he was—just that he was a white man. His stepfather, Washington Ferguson, lived on a neighboring farm.

It was common for one or more families to live together in crowded conditions.

Library of Congress

Booker lived in a cabin like this one as a young boy. His mother was the cook for the farm. She cooked 3 meals a day for 20 people. The kitchen cabin was also their sleeping quarters.

Harper's Encyclopedia

Booker got along well enough with his owners, who were not as cruel as some slave owners. James and Elizabeth Burroughs were not well-to-do, so they worked alongside their slaves. Even after slavery ended, Booker stayed in touch with them until they died. Like many slaves, he was poorly fed and clothed, overworked, and received no education. Every night, he slept on the cold, dirt floor of the cabin with only a pile of rags as a mattress.

In spite of the fact that his mother was the cook, Booker was often hungry. One of his early memories was of his mother roasting a stolen chicken for the family. Booker also liked to sneak a sweet potato out of the pit in the middle of the cabin floor when he could stand the hunger pains no longer. He hated the coarse linen shirts slave children had to wear. These were downright painful when they were new and felt like hundreds of sharp pins scratching the skin. Once his older brother, John, took Booker's new shirt and wore it a few days to break it in. Booker always remembered this kind act from his big brother.

The slaves on Booker's farm kept up with news of the Civil War by what they called "the grapevine." The man who picked up the mail every few days also brought home the latest gossip. In town he would stand around and overhear the talk of the white men. Many times, he would arrive home with the mail before his owner, and the other slaves would get the news first. This way they kept up with the battles and the progress of the Civil War.

Everyone knew that something big was going to happen soon. The slaves could feel the excitement in the air. They heard the war was almost over. Mr. Burroughs ordered them to bury the silver and other valuables in the yard. He did not want the Union soldiers to have them.

For the rest of his life, 9-year-old Booker remembered what happened the next day. The slaves were called together and a Union officer talked to them. Then he read the great document that President Lincoln wrote, the Emancipation Proclamation. Booker wrote:

> President Abraham Lincoln issued the famous **Emancipation Proclamation** on January 1, 1863. This document did free slaves, but only ones in the Confederate states still fighting the Union army. It also allowed blacks to serve as soldiers. Slavery was not totally outlawed in the United States until the **13th Amendment** to the Constitution was passed on December 18, 1865.

After the reading we were told that we were all free, and could go when and where we pleased. My mother, who was standing by my side, leaned over and kissed her children, while tears of joy ran down her cheeks. She explained to us what it all meant that this was the day for which she had been so long praying, but fearing she would never live to see. For some minutes there was great rejoicing, and thanksgiving, and wild scenes of ecstasy.

This famous painting shows President Lincoln after he wrote the Emancipation Proclamation. Booker was just a young boy when a Union soldier read this famous document to him and his family. His mother cried tears of joy when she heard the news.

Library of Congress

In his book *Up from Slavery,* Booker wrote that having freedom handed to you so suddenly was like telling a child that he had to take care of himself. Most blacks had no skills to earn a living other than the ones they had learned as slaves. But most were eager to try out their freedom by changing their names and leaving the plantation for a few days at least. Soon, many returned asking their former owner about working for pay.

Many freed blacks were interested in getting an education, voting, and running for public office. Some white people in the South were not only afraid of this; they were determined to stop it. This was when a secret society, the Ku Klux Klan, was formed.

This was a gang of white men who patrolled at night to terrorize and to control black people. They wore white robes and

> **The Ku Klux Klan, or KKK**, organized in 1865–66. The first leader was Nathan Bedford Forrest, a Confederate general. The group believed whites were superior to blacks and used violence to get what they wanted. Not until 1871 did Congress pass a law allowing President Ulysses S. Grant to use troops against the Klan.

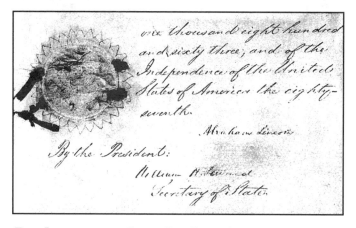

Booker remembered when Union soldiers read the Emancipation Proclamation. This document, signed by President Lincoln, freed the slaves in 1863.

hooded masks and burned crosses in yards of blacks. They also destroyed schools and burned churches. Many innocent black people were killed or tortured during these violent times.

As a boy, the Klan frightened Booker. One day he was an eyewitness to a racial riot in his town. A large crowd of blacks and whites broke into a vicious fight. Booker thought there were as many as 200 people and he was terrified. Even a white man who tried to defend the blacks was knocked down and seriously injured. There were no laws to protect black people from this violence, and those white people who felt this was wrong were often afraid to step in. It was a terrible time for black families in the South with widespread feelings of hatred.

After the war, Booker's stepfather found work in Malden, West Virginia, and sent for his family to come join him. It was several hundred miles to their new home and the family had to walk to get there. They put their few possessions into a cart and slept outdoors at night along their way.

Life in West Virginia was not easy. Booker was forced to work in the salt furnace with his stepfather, having to arise early in the morning. But one good thing hap-pened to Booker. He met a young man who could read the newspaper. Groups of people gathered around in the evenings to hear him read.

Booker desperately wanted to learn to read. He had been very curious about the schoolbooks of his young mistress on the farm in Virginia. About this time, his mother gave him his first book, an old Webster blue back spelling book. He studied it every minute he could.

The parents in Malden got together and hired a teacher for their children. Booker was very excited, but this soon turned to one of the biggest disappointments he ever had. His stepfather told him he would have to work

After the war, the Ku Klux Klan formed to keep black men from voting and holding office. The Klansmen wore long robes and hoods over their faces. They terrorized blacks by bullying them, breaking into their homes, and burning crosses in their yards. Many innocent blacks were killed after the war.

instead of going to school. The family needed the money. Everyday he could see the other children on their way to school and that made him even sadder.

Booker was determined he would not be left out. He walked several miles after work each day for lessons with a teacher. With the long walk home and having to report to work so early, there was little time for sleep. Booker believed it was worth it though because he wanted to learn.

For a while, he tried working and going to school, but he was always late to one or the other. When he started school, Booker heard the roll call for the first time. He noticed that the other children had a first name and a last name. He wondered what he should say. Though his mother had given him the name Taliaferro when he was born, all he had ever been called was Booker. When the teacher asked for his name he made a quick decision and chose Washington for his last name. Booker T. Washington was the name he used the rest of his life.

Most of the children at school wore hats, but Booker did not. Like most children, he wanted what other children had and he was embarrassed by his bare head. He begged his mother for a store-bought hat but she did not have enough money. Instead, she made him a homemade cap out of cloth scraps. Many of his classmates made fun of it. When he grew up, Booker said he was proud of his mother for using her money wisely and not wasting it on a popular but unneeded item.

Next, Booker's stepfather arranged for him to work in the coal mines. He hated this dangerous, dirty job. There were explosions and cave-ins that really frightened him. During this period, he heard about the Hampton Normal and Agricultural Institute of Virginia from two miners. Soon this was all he could think about. He was determined that one day he would go to this great school for blacks.

At about the same time, Booker heard about an opening for a job at the home of Gen. Lewis Ruffner, owner of the mine. His wife, Mrs. Viola Ruffner, needed a houseboy. Eager to leave the dark coal mine, Booker gladly took the position for $5 a month. Mrs. Ruffner had a reputation around town for being so strict that no one could work for her more than a couple of weeks. She was a fanatic about cleanliness and nobody could ever do the work well enough to please her.

Booker says he heard so much about her that he trembled when he went into her presence. Soon, he learned that she had a lot to teach him. He said:

The lessons I learned in the home of Mrs. Ruffner were as valuable to me as any education I have ever gotten anywhere since. Even to this day I never see bits of paper scattered around a house or in the street that I do not want to pick them up at once. I never see a filthy yard that I do not want to clean it, a paling off of a fence that I do not want to put it on, an unpainted or unwhitewashed house that I do not want to paint or whitewash it, or a button off one's clothes, or a grease-spot on them or on the floor that I do not want to call attention to it...

Little did he know that this training from old Mrs. Ruffner would help him later.

Between his earnings, some money from his brother, and donations from elderly neighbors, 16-year-old Booker decided he was ready to make the 500-mile trip to Hampton Institute. Not only did he have to pay a fee to enter school; he had to pay for his transportation. He packed a single bag with his old clothes and headed out to catch the trains and stagecoaches. Soon, he realized he did not have enough money.

There were other problems. At one stagecoach stop, he expected to get a room just like the other passengers. It never

Booker T. Washington as a young man
Rare Book Collection, University of
North Carolina-Chapel Hill

crossed his mind that the color of his skin would matter. The innkeeper refused to give him food or a room, and he spent the night walking around outside until the stagecoach left the next morning. Now penniless, Booker hitched rides on wagons and cars, or he walked.

He finally made it to Richmond, Virginia, late at night without any money and not knowing a single person. He remembered:

> I passed by many food-stands where fried chicken and half-moon apple pies were piled high....At that time it seemed to me that I would have promised all...to have gotten hold of one of those chicken legs or one of those pies.

Wandering the street in complete exhaustion, Booker finally crawled under a wooden sidewalk to sleep and used his suitcase as a pillow. The next morning he saw a large ship and asked the captain for a job unloading the cargo. Booker stayed in Richmond several days working for the captain and sleeping under the same sidewalk. As soon as he had enough money to enroll in school, he continued on to Hampton. He arrived with only a few coins in his pocket.

The teacher in charge of admittance to the school was not too impressed with Booker. He had not taken a bath or changed his clothes in many days. She ignored him; nevertheless, he kept hanging around. After several hours of this she realized he was not going to leave. So she asked him to sweep one of the classrooms.

Booker knew this was his big chance to impress the teacher. All the lessons he had learned while cleaning and working for Mrs. Ruffner were about to pay off. He was suddenly glad she had been so picky. He not only swept the room, he did it 3 times in addition to dusting all the furniture, closets, and corners. The teacher came in and used her handkerchief to inspect. Finding not a speck of dirt, she told Booker he could enroll in the school. In his book he said that of all the exams he ever took, this was the best one he ever passed.

When Booker enrolled at Hampton, he was put in a room with 7 other boys. He did not quite know what to make of his bed, or what to do with the sheets. The first night he tried sleeping under both of the sheets but that did not seem right. So the second night he slept on top of them. Finally, he decided to watch what the other students did and he figured out how to properly use the sheets.

Throughout his years at Hampton, Booker worked as a janitor to pay his school fees. This meant cleaning at night when classes ended and rising at 4 a.m. to get the fires going and to study. One winter when the dormitories were overcrowded, he and other students slept in bitter-cold tents on the school grounds. Gen. Samuel Armstrong, head of the school, was a big influence in Booker's life. He was a very kind, compassionate, and highly intelligent man dedicated to helping free blacks get an education. His example is probably what later inspired Booker to become a teacher himself.

Booker worked hard and performed well in school. During this time, he formed a lot of his own ideas about life. He did not have any patience with people who made excuses. He said he "began everything with the idea he could succeed." Booker used his lunch periods to study and to practice debating. When summer vacation came, he could not afford to go home and visit his family like the other students. This made him sad, but he knew he must stay to finish his education.

When graduation time came, Booker was among the top students, finishing with honors. After this, he felt his life was a mission to help improve the conditions of his race. He often said, "Those who are happiest are those who do the most for others." He returned to his hometown in West Virginia to teach. Later, he was invited back to Hampton Normal School to teach a group of Kiowa and Cheyenne Indians.

In 1881, the town of Tuskegee, Alabama, was looking for a principal for a new free school for blacks. They wrote to General Armstrong. He immediately recommended Booker, who was only 25 years old at the time.

When he arrived, he received the news that there were no buildings, supplies, or land for his new school. He had $2,000 for teachers' salaries and that was it. Booker was discouraged, but not for long. He held the first classes in a shack owned by the African Methodist Episcopal Church. Soon, he borrowed $200 to make a down payment on a farm outside of town.

Booker allowed students to work for their school fees. Soon, he and the students were working from dawn to sundown repairing the run-down buildings. He often said, "One should measure success by the obstacles one overcomes." Rarely are men able to accomplish goals as difficult as the ones Booker set for himself. Through untiring work, bake sales, suppers, and fund-raising tours, Booker built the Tuskegee Institute.

When there was no kitchen, he and his students dug one out of the dirt basement of a farm building. At that time, he remembers students arguing over the coffee cup; there was only one for the whole school.

In a few short years, the Tuskegee Institute was famous all across the United States. Booker taught his students many things they had never learned when they were enslaved. He started with lessons as simple as how to set a table, eat a meal, and brush your teeth.

> In 1974, the **Tuskegee Institute** became a national historic site by vote of the U.S. Congress.

He also believed that students should recognize the value of physical labor. He taught them the latest in

This is a classroom at Booker T. Washington's famous Tuskegee Institute. Notice the clothing of the students. Booker insisted the students be well dressed for class. He would not approve of today's blue jeans and T-shirts.

Library of Congress

farming methods and provided them with skills they could use to obtain jobs. He told his students that most people appreciate hard work. His advice for success for these freed blacks was to "learn to do an uncommon thing in an uncommon manner."

The success of the school continued because Booker was constantly raising money. Many times he was afraid he could not pay his bills, but he never let his fear stop the work of the school. He used his own money, borrowed from friends, and even sold his own possessions, including a gold watch. One wealthy gentleman he asked for a donation gave him $2. Booker said at that moment he decided he would make this man so impressed with his school that he would want to give much more. Years later, Collis P. Huntington donated $50,000 for a new building named in his honor. Many wealthy people gave funds over the years making Tuskegee Institute one of the best-supported black schools in U.S. history.

In August of 1895, Booker received a great honor. He was invited to speak at the Cotton States and International Exposition in Atlanta, Georgia. It was one of the most important speeches of his life. Never had a black man been asked to speak to a crowd of Southern white people. In his speech, he hoped to create a spirit of friendship between the races. At the end, the audience leaped to their feet clapping and cheering. Some even threw their hats in the air and waved their canes. The newspapers discussed his speech for days to come and called it the Atlanta Compromise.

Booker was criticized for his speech and his attitudes in later years. Many blacks thought he should have spoken more forcefully for their cause and the right to vote. But Booker had his own way of doing things. In 1901, Booker's autobiography, *Up From Slavery,* was published. In it, he told his life story and his ideas. He believed the most important goal for blacks was self-improvement. He often said in speaking of his past that "Great men cultivate love; little men cherish the spirit of hatred."

Whether blacks agreed with Booker's philosophy or not, one thing was clear. Frederick Douglass died the same year that Booker made his Atlanta speech. The reins of leadership had been passed. The

Portrait of Booker T. Washington
Library of Congress

little boy who rode through the dark woods with his bag of corn was now the most famous black American in the country.

———————————

You may visit Booker's birthplace and childhood home at the Booker T. Washington National Monument in Hardy, Virginia (call 540-721-2094, or visit the website at http://www.nps.gov/bowa*); and the Tuskegee Institute National Historic Site in Alabama (call 334-727-3200, or visit the website at* http://www.nps.gov*). Both historic sites are operated by the National Park Service.*

Chapter 7

A Woman in the Regiment
Susie King Taylor (1848–1912)

Susie was under water and her lungs felt as if they would burst. The foamy waves crashed around her head, pushing her deeper and deeper into the dark ocean. She knew she had to fight if she was going to live. Struggling with her tired and aching arms, she forced herself to swim to the surface.

The churning ocean knocked her under a second time, and the strong salty foam went up her nose and choked her. She was starting to panic. What if she died out here in this cold, black water? She would never see her husband again. She was on the way to visit him when the accident happened.

Susie had climbed aboard the yacht around eight o'clock that evening with a small handful of passengers and a lone Union soldier. The plan was to sail to Beaufort, South Carolina. Her husband, Sgt. Edward King of Company E of the Union army, was stationed near there with his fellow soldiers. The famous Union Gen. William Tecumseh Sherman was not far away either. He had just captured Fort McAllister in Georgia.

They were on board only a few minutes when their boat overturned and they were cast into the ocean. The other 3 women on the voyage were struggling in the water. The corporal's wife, Mrs. Walker, was nearly hysterical. Her 2-year-old child was overboard. She reached for her baby while trying to hang onto the boat.

When Susie came up the second time, she grabbed the sail and held tight. Trapped underneath was the soldier, drowned. Susie and the other women screamed for help. No one seemed to hear their cries. Their arms and legs were growing cold and numb from being in the water so long.

Shortly before midnight, two boats from nearby Ladies Island heard them and came to their rescue. For Mrs. Walker, the help was too late. Her baby's lifeless body floated beside her in the water.

Susie finally made it back to camp but not before several weeks of recovery under the care of a doctor. Her brush with death was just one of many stories she had to tell after her 4-year service with the Union army during the Civil War. Fortunately for us, she decided some years later to write a book about slavery and her army life. This is how we know so much about her.

William Tecumseh Sherman, the Union general. Susie's husband was nearby when Sherman's troops took Fort McAllister.

Library of Congress

Childhood Memories

Although Susie grew up under Georgia slave laws, she was more fortunate than many young black girls born in 1848. Her owner, Mrs. Grest, took a personal interest in her. Susie and her brother sometimes slept on the foot of Mrs. Grest's bed when her husband was away on business trips. When Susie was 7, her Grandmother Dolly asked the Grests whether she could take the children from their island farm to live in Savannah with her. She was very surprised and happy when they said yes.

Susie had a better quality of life with Grandmother Dolly than she did as a slave. Her grandmother was a free black. She ran a trading business, washed laundry, and cleaned rooms for boarders. Dolly had more money than many black people did at that time.

There was another reason Susie was glad to be with her grandmother. Each month, she saw troops of 40 or more slaves marching on their way to be sold. From her grandmother's porch, she could hear the voice of the auctioneer selling the slaves one by one. It was a frightening sound.

Grandmother Dolly knew how important it was to get an education. One of her friends, Mrs. Woodhouse, was also free. Even though it was against the law, she ran a school in her home for nearly 30 black children.

Every morning, Susie's stomach tightened into a knot. She and the other students had to hide their books and sneak into Mrs. Woodhouse's kitchen where class was held. If they were caught with books, they would be severely punished.

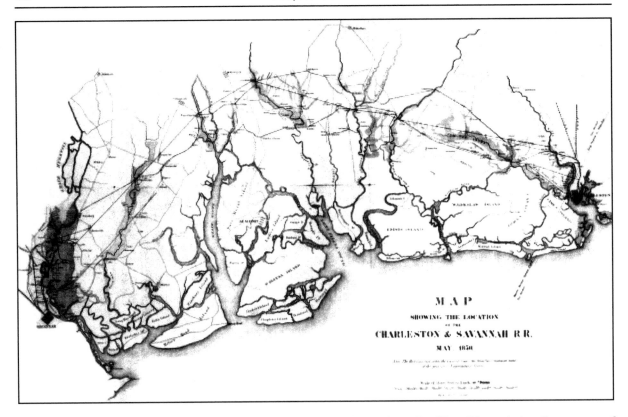

M A P

SHOWING THE LOCATION

CHARLESTON & SAVANNAH R.R.

MAY 1850

Susie grew up in Savannah with her Grandmother Dolly. She visited many of these coastal islands during her years as a war nurse and laundress.

Library of Congress

Susie was a very bright student. Her grandmother had to find more teachers for her because she learned so fast. One of Susie's teachers was a neighborhood play-mate, a white child named Katie O'Connor. Katie must have been very fond of Susie. She told Susie she would teach her every night if she promised never to tell Katie's father. Sadly, this lasted just a few short months. This part of Susie's education ended suddenly when Katie's parents sent her to a convent.

Because she could write well, Susie became very popular. At that time, all black people were required to have a written pass to travel, especially at night. Slaves had to have passes signed by their owners. Even the free blacks were required to have a guardian who could write the slips for them. Any blacks without passes could be arrested. Pretty soon, Susie was quite good at writing passes for Grandmother Dolly and faking her guardian's signature.

Like many young black girls, Susie heard tales about the Yankees. She wondered just what one of these myste-rious creatures looked like. She knew from listening to her grandmother that Yankees would free the slaves. But

> Wording of a fake **pass**: "Pass the bearer—From 9–10:30 P.M.—Valen-tine Grest—Savannah, Ga., March 1, 1860."

A building for holding slaves, like this one, was near Susie's grandmother's home in Savannah, Georgia. Troops of slaves marched by on their way to be sold.

Library of Congress

Slave auctions were held here. As a young girl, Susie could hear the auctioneer from her grandmother's porch.

Library of Congress

Enslaved blacks were required to have a written pass from their owners when they traveled. Failure to have this important piece of paper meant instant punishment.

Frank Leslie's *Our Soldier in the Civil War*

she was confused because white people told her something completely different. They said she should be afraid of them—Yankees took little girls like her, tied them to carts, and treated them like horses.

Susie did not have to wait long to meet a real live Yankee. She was visiting her mother in the countryside when the Union forces took Fort Pulaski, Georgia, in 1862. She was terribly frightened of the loud noise of the guns and the way the ground shook. When the Yankees won, Susie's life changed forever. She was now safely under

Yankee—A nickname for a Union solder.
Rebel—A nickname for a Confederate soldier.

the protection of the Union army. The soldiers would soon be taking her and other black families to nearby St. Simon's Island to begin their new life of freedom.

Susie Becomes a Teacher and a Nurse

The commanding officers saw right away what a bright, talented young woman Susie was. On board a ship to the island, Captain Whitmore questioned Susie. He was shocked that she knew how to read and write so well. She also stitched a few napkins for him to show off her sewing skills. He had never met a black woman who could do such things. Whitmore took this news to Commodore Goldsborough.

Susie was on a nearby sea island when Fort Pulaski was captured. The big cannons were so loud and powerful they made the ground shake. Her life changed forever when the Union soldiers set her free.

Frank Leslie's *Our Soldier in the Civil War*

Susie heard the big guns during the battle at Fort Pulaski. After that, she worked with Union soldiers as a nurse and laundress.

Library of Congress, Photograph by Mathew Brady

Imagine Susie's surprise when Goldsborough named her the teacher for all the children on St. Simon's Island. She had nearly 40 students! Many of the adults came to her after school, too. Having been told for so long that they could not read, the freed blacks were so excited and happy about this chance to learn.

Susie's position as teacher did not last for long. The Union soldiers received orders to evacuate the island to Beaufort. The officer in charge took many of the freed blacks and enlisted them in the army. Susie was signed on to do the laundry for the soldiers.

For the next 4 years, Susie served with the 33rd U.S. Colored Troops, also known as the late 1st South Carolina Volunteers. They saw military action in 11 battles over a period of 2 years. They were stationed on many islands in lower South Carolina and Georgia.

During the war, Susie King Taylor served as a teacher, nurse, and laundress. She wrote the only known book by a black Civil War nurse.
Courtesy of South Carolina State Library

Like other black soldiers, they were not paid. Instead, their wives earned money by washing and baking pies to sell. In 1863, the government changed its rule and offered half pay to black soldiers. The soldiers in Susie's regiment were angry! They decided to take no pay at all until they were given full wages like everyone else. At the end of the war, the government paid them back at the full rate, but it did not erase some angry feelings of not being treated with respect.

Even their first uniforms were not the same as the white soldiers. The army expected them to wear old red ones that made them easy targets for the Rebels. They were no longer slaves, but they were still not treated equally.

Although Susie was the official laundress, she quickly learned to do any job when asked. She served as a nurse and a teacher, and even came close to military action. In the winter of 1863, mild cases of smallpox broke out among the troops. This was a deadly germ. One young soldier named

> **Smallpox** was a highly infectious disease with high fevers and pockmarks on the skin. Soldiers in the Civil War were far more likely to die of disease than injuries.

Here the 1st South Carolina Volunteers drill at Hilton Head Island, South Carolina. At first, President Lincoln wondered if blacks should serve in the armed forces. But these men became loyal, brave soldiers and proved him wrong.

Frank Leslie's *Our Soldier in the Civil War*

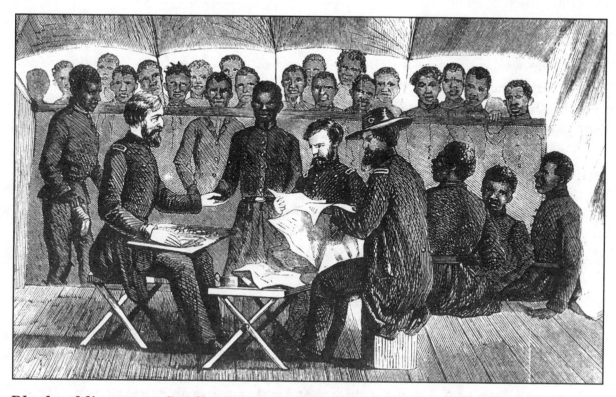

Black soldiers were finally given a chance to serve in the Union army.

Harper's *Illustrated History of the Great Rebellion*

Edward had a terrible case, and everyone was afraid to go near him. Not Susie—she showed up at his tent every day to nurse him back to health.

At one time, Susie's regiment was stationed at Camp Shaw, named after the famous Colonel Robert Gould Shaw of the 54th Massachusetts Infantry. This all-black regiment fought in a battle at Fort Wagner near Charleston, South Carolina, in 1863. When attacking the fort on foot, nearly half of their soldiers and Colonel Shaw were brutally killed. But they held the fort for nearly an hour before they were slaughtered.

This was the first time blacks were given a chance to really prove themselves in combat. Because of their bravery, all black soldiers were treated with respect after this. This battle was a history-making moment for blacks. Even in modern times, this event is remembered. An Oscar-winning major motion picture, *Glory,* was made about these soldiers in 1989.

Life in Camp

During her years in the war, Susie experienced ordinary life in military camp as well as more dangerous days. She would never forget her stay at Camp Shaw when the regiment was ordered to Jacksonville. While there, Susie's life was in terrible danger. The fighting grew nearer and nearer. The Rebel shelling came so close to her quarters, the colonel sent her into town to stay at the hospital. The rest of her life she remembered what it was like to have enemy fire come so close.

But Susie had the opportunity to be near friendly soldiers too. While on Seabrook Island, she was allowed to walk along the picket lines. She says she could see the Rebel soldiers across the river. Sometimes the soldiers would yell friendly hellos over to each other asking for food or tobacco. A few crossed over and deserted saying that they had "no negroes to fight for."

One of Susie's memories was a mail mix-up. Once, the 1st South Carolina Volunteers received the mail for the Confederates, and the Confederates received the mail for them. Captain L. W. Metcalf, of the 1st South Carolina Volunteers, sailed across the river under a flag of truce to swap the letters. He shook hands and visited with the Confederate soldiers there before returning. Although they were enemies, soldiers from both sides still treated each other as fellow human beings.

Although women usually never did such a thing back then, Susie learned to handle a gun during her time in the army. She said:

> I learned to handle a musket very well while in the regiment, and could shoot straight and often hit the target. I assisted in cleaning the guns and used to fire them off, to see if the cartridges were dry, before cleaning and reloading, each day. I thought this great fun. I was also able to take a gun all apart and put it together again.

This is the U.S. Federal Hospital at Hilton Head Island, South Carolina. Susie helped tend sick and wounded soldiers during her years in the war.

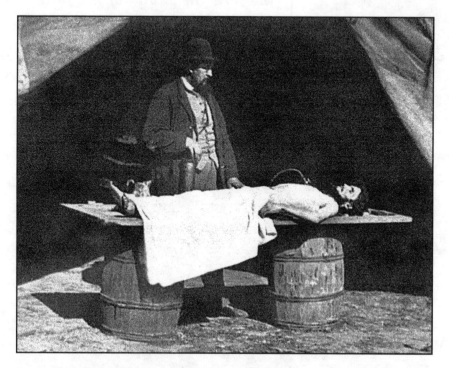

A Civil War surgeon prepares the body of a dead soldier. As a war nurse, Susie saw many sights like this.

(Above) *The monument to the 54th Massachusetts all-black regiment*

Library of Congress

(Left) *Colonel Robert Gould Shaw led an all-black regiment, the 54th Massachusetts. When he led the attack on Fort Wagner, he died there along with half of his men. When Susie visited the fort, the skulls of the fallen soldiers still covered the ground.*

Harper's Weekly

(Below) *When Port Royal and Beaufort, South Carolina, were captured, the Union army began to use black soldiers.*

Frank Leslie's *Our Soldier in the Civil War*

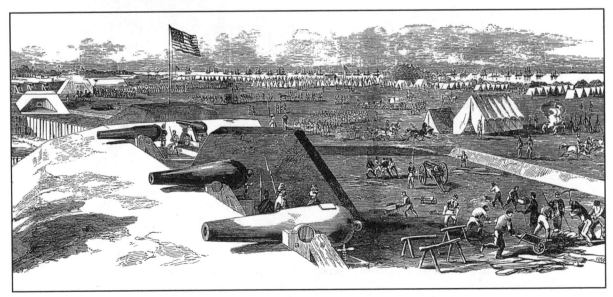

The 1st South Carolina Volunteers fire on the Confederates. They were eager to prove that black men would make excellent soldiers. These were the first black troops in U.S. history.

Frank Leslie's *Our Soldier in the Civil War*

For a young black woman, Susie was seeing and doing things out of the ordinary. There was a lot of excitement when a spy was captured at Beaufort. Susie was there when he was placed on top of his own coffin on a wagon and marched through town. The colonel did this to frighten other soldiers who were thinking of spying. The soldiers took the traitor to the back of camp and shot him. Susie said, "I shall never forget this scene."

In later years, Susie wrote her memories in a book called *Reminiscences of My Life in Camp*. From her writings, a lot was learned about the details of ordinary army life such as food. Union soldiers not only had more food than the Confederates did, it was better too. The Confederates were running out of supplies because of the Union blockades. Susie said they had fresh beef occasionally but usually salt-beef.

Blockade—Blocking ships with food and supplies from reaching the enemy. Twenty-five out of every 100 men in the Union navy were free blacks or former slaves.

When the Emancipation Proclamation was read, the troops feasted on several roasted oxen. Dried vegetable soup, pancakes, tea, and hardtack were the foods eaten most of the time. During one difficult battle when the

Hardtack—A hard, dry biscuit made of flour and water.

food was nearly gone, Susie made custard from turtle eggs for the sick soldiers.

Susie learned how to keep warm during the winter. She took a cooking pan lined with dirt and filled it with hot coals. Once she was in her tent, she could cover this with another pan so it did not make any light. After taps, no one wanted the enemy spotting him because of light in his tent.

Once the cold weather passed, the bugs moved in. Susie spent one long night sitting up with a friend. Neither of them could sleep because the fleas were so thick.

> **Taps**—A bugle call signaling lights out in camp.
> **Reveille**—A bugle call signaling the start of the soldier's day.

While stationed near Fort Wagner, Susie liked to go there to watch the firing on Charleston. The grounds of the fort were covered with skulls so thick she had to move them aside to walk on the paths. She wondered whether any of them were black soldiers. She remembered:

> They were a gruesome sight these fleshless heads and grinning jaws, but by this time I had become accustomed to worse things. It seems strange...how we are able to see the most sickening sights, such as men with their limbs blown off and mangled by deadly shells without a shudder; and instead of turning away, how we hurry to (help ease) their pain, bind up their wounds and press the cool water to their parched lips with feelings only of sympathy and pity.

Susie walked across bones and skulls of fallen soldiers at Fort Wagner. This man is gathering remains from a Civil War battlefield.

Library of Congress

During a visit to Beaufort, Susie met the famous Civil War nurse Clara Barton, who later started the American Red Cross. She made a big impression on Susie who watched how she cared for the wounded soldiers. What she learned from the famous nurse helped her back at camp.

Even in the middle of all the fighting and suffering, the soldiers found time for fun. A soldier, who was marching North, gave a pig to Colonel Charles T. Trowbridge. The colonel decided to bring it into camp. Quickly, "Piggie" became a pet. The drummer boys were especially fond of him, teaching him tricks. More than once they got in trouble for riding him in the middle of the evening camp meetings. Soon "Piggie" learned how to march in time at dress parade.

Clara Barton, the famous Civil War nurse, later founded the American Red Cross. Susie met her in South Carolina. She learned a lot about caring for wounded soldiers.

National Archives

Sights and Sounds of Charleston

In the last months of the war, Susie's regiment was ordered to Charleston, South Carolina. The Rebels, realizing they would have to leave the city, decided to set it on fire. The black soldiers were given the job of fighting the fires. They were able to save many buildings and lives, but some of the white citizens were not grateful for the help of former slaves. Susie stayed in a fancy home on South Battery Street. Here she helped set up a hospital for the wounded and sick. Today, this is a popular area for Charleston tourists.

After the Charleston assignment, Susie's regiment came into contact with a dangerous criminal. The soldiers were marching in the countryside between Hamburg and Charleston. The bushwhackers, as soldiers fighting in the woods were sometimes called, were very good at hiding and surprising the soldiers coming through. One daring bushwhacker had everyone afraid to go to sleep. No one knew his identity. He would wait until the dark of night when the soldiers fell asleep in the train cars that would move them the next day. Then into the train he would creep, silent as a cat, as he slit their throats. Many men died this way. One night, an alert guard caught the murderer in the act. He was arrested and shot at Wall Hollow.

A view of the ruins of Charleston, South Carolina. Susie was with Union forces when they entered the city. When Charleston was set on fire, black soldiers helped put out the flames.

Library of Congress

The End Draws Near

In the next weeks, Susie's regiment was returned to Morris Island. There they received the news that they were being "mustered out," or discharged from, the army. Susie recalls the reaction of the troops and their friendship with their white colonel:

They were delighted to go home, but oh! How they hated to part from their commanding chief, Colonel C. T. Trowbridge. He was the very first officer to take charge of black soldiers. We thought there was no one like him, for he was a "man" among his soldiers. All in the regiment knew him personally, and many were the jokes he used to tell them. I shall never forget his friendship and kindness toward me, from the first time I met him to the end of the war.

Colonel Trowbridge gathered his troops to bid them farewell. He told them there was not a better spot for this to happen. They were gathered near the unmarked graves of the courageous soldiers of the 54th Massachusetts Regiment. He spoke:

Comrades: The hour is at hand when we must separate forever, and nothing can take from us the pride we feel, when we look upon the history of the

"First South Carolina Volunteers", the first black regiment that ever bore arms in defense of freedom on the continent of America....In the face of the floods of prejudice, you came forth to do battle for your country and kindred. For long and weary months, without pay or even the privilege of being recognized as soldiers, you labored on....From that little band of hopeful, trusting and brave men, amidst the terrible prejudices that surrounded us, has grown an army of a hundred and forty thousand black soldiers, whose valor and heroism has won for your race a name which will live as long as the undying pages of history shall endure; and by whose efforts....to remove forever the possibility of human slavery being established within the borders of redeemed America.

By the end of the Civil War, 180,000 blacks were Union soldiers.

After the war, Susie continued to teach. Sadly, her sergeant husband died not long after that, and she moved North. While in Boston, she married Russell L. Taylor in 1879. Still interested in the lives of military men, she helped form a Women's Relief Auxiliary to aid the former soldiers. In the Spanish-American War, she helped furnish supplies for the troops. Many black soldiers also served in that war. She was always seeking to improve the quality of life, something she wrote about at the end of her book:

Now, despite all the hindrances and "race problems," my people are striving to attain the full standard of all other races born free in the sight of God, and in a number of instances have succeeded. Justice, we ask—to be citizens of these United States, where so many of our people have shed their blood with their white comrades, that the stars and stripes should never be polluted.

Susie spent her early years enslaved on a Georgia farm, but she went on to serve in one of the most famous regiments in the Civil War. She died in 1912, but today people still remember her troops as the first black soldiers to organize, drill and bear arms. She stood on the ground where the soldiers of the 54th Massachusetts died, proving that black men were worthy to fight in this war that set them free. When Susie signed on to do the soldiers' laundry, she never dreamed she would be making history for her people.

If you visit Savannah, Georgia, arrange a visit to the King-Tisdell Cottage Foundation, Inc., at 502 East Harris Street. Call 912-234-8000 for information, or visit the website at http://www.kingtisdell.org. Here you may learn more about black heritage in Savannah, where Susie King Taylor spent her childhood years.

Chapter 8

Deadwood Dick and the Wild, Wild West
Nat Love (1854–1925)

Nat was hanging on for dear life. Never had this 11-year-old boy had such a wild ride. The big black stallion underneath him thrashed, churned, and bucked as hard as he could. Every bone in Nat's body was rattled and pounded as he was slammed onto the back of the horse over and over again.

Dust from the barnyard flew everywhere, and his nose and lungs were clogged and choked with flying dirt. Any minute, Nat expected to fly into the air and hit the ground. He hated to admit it, but he was afraid. Everyone knew that Black Highwayman was a bad-tempered horse. But Nat was full of mischief and he loved excitement. When his friends dared him to ride the black stallion, he could not resist. Now, he was wondering whether he made a big mistake.

For several weeks now, Nat had been sneaking over to Mr. Williams's ranch. His sons, who were close to Nat's age, had a job for him. They said they would pay him 10¢ for every wild horse he broke. But he had to do it on Sunday mornings when the family was at church, so their father would not find out. Nat could not resist having some money of his own. So far, he had successfully broken 12 colts.

For breaking Black Highwayman, he insisted on more pay. After arguing awhile, the boys settled on 25¢. Nat got his payment in advance and knotted his coin into a corner of his shirt for safekeeping. Once on top of the wild, thrashing horse, he wished he had held out for 50¢.

Suddenly, Black Highwayman bolted and jumped over the garden fence. All the noise stirred up the dogs that decided to chase. Farther and farther the black stallion

91

ran, jumping over everything in his path. More and more dogs were joining the pack in hot pursuit. Neighbors saw Nat speeding by and jumped on their horses to follow. It seemed as if the whole town was out chasing down the wild horse. The men tried to grab the horse and stop him. But Nat was riding without a saddle or bridle so it was no use.

Nat clung to the horse as hard as he could, his knuckles holding the thick black mane. He knew he had to stay there until Black Highwayman gave in. Finally, the exhausted horse realized he had met his match. As he slowed to a halt, Nat reached for his reward for all this trouble. His heart sank in disappointment as he felt the corner of his shirt. Black Highwayman had bucked loose the knot in his shirt and his 25¢ was gone. To top it all, now he was going to be in trouble with Mr. Williams for creating such a commotion on Sunday. Suddenly, he wished he never took that dare.

Much later in life, Nat would write his autobiography. His story gives us a clear picture of what his childhood was like during the Civil War and the hard years after the war. He also tells what he and other young boys did to entertain themselves.

Nat's family was living on Mr. Robert Love's Tennessee plantation when he was born in June of 1854. His sister, Sally, was 8, and his brother, Jordan, was 5 at the time. His parents were very important slaves. His father was the foreman, and his mother was the cook for her owner. She also had other jobs including milking the cows and running the loom to weave clothes for all the slaves. Sally's main job was to fan the flies from the dining table. She also helped her mother.

Nat Love grew up in conditions like this. When he was not working, he and his friends pretended to be Yankee soldiers. He often invented his own fun organizing rabbit hunts for the other boys.

Slave owners often housed many blacks together in one cabin. This photo was taken on a South Carolina plantation.

The man who owned Nat's father put him in charge. It was his job to make sure everyone worked hard every day.

With all of his family so busy, Nat pretty much looked after himself. Early on, he showed a talent for doing fun but dangerous things. If nothing interesting was going on, Nat created his own excitement. He liked to raid the garden for watermelons and sweet potatoes even though he knew he would be punished if caught.

He and the other boys often engaged in "rock battles." This dangerous game consisted of two teams of boys trying to stone each other. The boys took the competition quite seriously, taking aim to hit their opponents. The losing team had to turn and run to keep from being seriously hurt. Once, a child was nearly killed, and all the boys got whippings from their parents. Rock battles were forbidden after that.

Not content to lead a boring life, next Nat organized a rabbit hunt. He and the neighborhood boys gathered up the hunting dogs to chase the rabbits. Nat remembered running through the brambles and thorns with only a shirt on and his shirttails flying. Most of the young slave boys did not own or wear pants or shoes. At the end of the hunt, their legs were covered with bloody scratches, but they did not care. They chased the dogs and rabbits as long as they would run.

Although Nat remembers his owner as kind, he saw other slaves receive vicious whippings. It upset him that he and the other slaves could not get an education. He remembered seeing slaves sold at auction and hearing the sad cries among family members as they were separated.

When Nat was 10, the Civil War started. Most enslaved people knew enough to understand that the outcome of the war would be important to them. They talked of little else. The children were caught up in the excitement too. Nat's father went with Mr. Love when he signed on as a soldier. Nat's job was to help General Robert E. Lee build forts. Of course, Nat and the other slave boys wanted to be soldiers. So Nat decided to form his own "army."

When all the boys were in a group, Nat started dividing them up into Rebels and Yankees. The boys loudly yelled their protest. Not one of them wanted to be a Rebel! So the Yanks were forced to march into the countryside to find another enemy. They did not have to wait long. There were plenty of insects to fight. With the yellow jackets, they named the battle, the capture of Fort Hell.

> In remembering how slaves were treated, Nat wrote: **"As young as I was my blood often boiled as I witnessed these cruel sights...the most sacred commands of God were violated under the law of the land."**

> **Rebel** was the nickname for soldiers fighting for the states in the **Confederacy**, or South. **Yankee** was the nickname for soldiers fighting for the **Union**, or North. Robert E. Lee was the commanding general of the Rebels, and Ulysses S. Grant was the general of the Yanks. Nat's father worked for Lee, and Grant's troops marched through Nat's neighborhood.

The Battle of the Wilderness and the bombing of Fort Sumter were against bumble-bees and hornets.

The hardest battle that these young soldiers fought was against a large nest of wasps. Nat remembered:

> We attacked with cheers, only to be driven back time and again and finally we...[made] a retreat at full speed in the direction of home...We secured more ammunition, in the shape of old rags, brooms...and returned to the

(Left) *General Robert E. Lee*

Library of Congress

(Below) *Nat Love's father went to war with his owner and built forts for General Robert E. Lee. Even in the North, black men were not allowed to fight until later in the war. Notice the drawing style in this picture. If someone today drew black people in this way, it would be considered racist. Back then, it was done a lot. The style is known as caricature, where a person's features or clothes are exaggerated.*

Frank Leslie's *Our Soldier in the Civil War*

charge...although we were driven back several times we stayed until we won out, and the last insect lay a quivering mass on the ground. The Union forces were victorious and we were happy.

Nat's nose was terribly swollen, and he could not use his eyes for several days. Nevertheless, in his mind he won a war and defeated the enemy.

To keep his slaves at home, Mr. Love put out the word that the Union soldiers would hang any slaves they caught. Of course, this frightened Nat and his friends. When General Ulysses S. Grant arrived in the neighborhood, the slaves found that the Union soldiers were friendly enough. The troops did, however, take all the available food as they marched through on their way south to fight. Many families went hungry after they left.

(Left) *General Ulysses S. Grant*

Library of Congress

(Below) *The Union troops of Ulysses S. Grant marched through Nat Love's community on their way south. Nat's owner told him the soldiers would hang him if they caught him. He found they were friendly but they took all the food on the way through. Many people were hungry after that.*

Harper's Weekly

When slaves on the farm heard the news of General Lee's surrender, they knew the war was ending. Soon, Mr. Love returned home, and life went back to usual. Nat said, "In common with other masters (owners) of those days he did not tell us we were free." Mr. Love moved their cabin to a nearby hill and made the slaves keep working for him. A long time passed before they got the exciting news of their freedom. Then, there was plenty of celebrating and rejoicing.

Nat's father was a hardworking man and wanted his family to have a better life. Instead of continuing to work for Mr. Love as a lot of free blacks did, he rented 20 acres. His early years of farming were very hard. The family was often hungry, eating bran and cracklings. Nat's mother sometimes made ashcake, a thin batter of bran and water baked in cabbage leaves and hot coals. Nat and his brothers helped his father make straw mats, brooms, and cane chair seats to sell.

After tending to the corn and tobacco crops by day, Nat's father taught the family their ABCs in the evening. He was a strong person willing to do everything he could for his family whom he loved so much. After the war, the living conditions all across the South were terrible for people, black and white alike. Nat's father never let his family become discouraged during these years of poverty.

After the war, Nat's father wanted a better life for his family. He rented land from his former owner to grow his own crops. In spite of all their hard work, they were very poor and hungry.

Library of Congress

After the second crop was harvested, Nat's family had a terrible blow. His father became seriously ill and died. Shortly after this, his sister's husband died too. Nat suddenly found himself in charge of the family. He took a job on a nearby farm for $1.50 a week. The job did not last long. Mr. Brooks, his employer, tried to cheat Nat and only paid him 50¢ for a month's work. Nat got into a fistfight with him.

Next, Nat's family gathered berries and nuts for money. Once after a long day's work, they discovered some stray pigs had eaten all the blackberries. Nat's poor mother broke down and cried. Remembering how his father refused to be discouraged, Nat returned to the woods right then and worked until dark to fill the baskets. He said this difficult time in his life helped make him a strong, independent person.

> **Reconstruction** was the period of healing and rebuilding after the Civil War. It lasted 1865–1877. Our country tried to come together again. Northern factories were still operating, but Southern cities and railroads were destroyed during the years of fighting. There was severe poverty for a long time. Nat's family suffered terribly during these years. Many blacks were no better off with their new freedom. They had no money and no education. Many Southern states enacted laws to deny black people any rights such as voting and holding office.

Fifteen-year-old Nat was finding it harder and harder to feed his family. He began to daydream about exploring the rest of the world and getting an education. Stories of cowboys and the Wild West filled his head. Soon, he had his chance at a horse raffle. He could hardly believe his ears when his number was called. Nat sold the horse and took half the money home to his mother. The other half he planned to use to travel.

Nat's mother was sad that he wanted to go West, but she did not stop him. He convinced his uncle to come live with his mother and brother and to help them farm. Soon 15-year-old Nat left his home near Nashville, Tennessee, and headed for Dodge City, Kansas.

Nat arrived at a town full of cowboys and saloons. He had never seen anything like the dance halls, girls, and gamblers. He found a group of cowboys who were heading back to Texas soon and told them he wanted to go with them. Bronko Jim agreed to give him a job if he could ride a wild horse. Nat just smiled and remembered old Black Highwayman.

The cowboys brought out Good Eye, known to be the toughest bucking horse around. Nat said it was the worst horse he ever rode in his life, but he managed to hold on. After he passed the test, Bronko Jim gave him a new name: Red River Dick.

From 1869 to 1890, Nat lived the life of a cowboy in the Wild West. All his life, he loved danger and excitement. He had plenty of it in his new work in the West. His first day, a band of 100 Indians attacked the cowboys on the trail. The man riding next to Nat was shot off his horse and killed.

Over the years, Nat was involved in many Indian fights and shootouts with cattle rustlers. Once he was captured by a band of Indians, who held him prisoner for more than a month. He fought his captors, killing several of them and wounding many others. The chief was impressed that he was such a strong, brave man and decided Nat should marry his daughter. One night, Nat stole one of their fastest ponies and made his getaway just in time.

> Nearly 20 million buffalo once roamed the wild, Wild West. Overhunting nearly caused them to become **extinct,** or die out. There were only 500 in existence by 1889.

Once on a cattle drive, Nat saw a buffalo stampede. "All at once, we became aware of a roaring noise in the north like thunder, slowly growing louder as it approached." Nat and the other cowboys tried their best to keep the hundreds of buffalo from going through the herd of cattle. He said, "They paid no more attention to us than they would have paid to a lot of boys with pea shooters." The horse of a cowboy named Cal Surcey panicked and ran in front of the herd. Nat saw Cal go down and the whole herd trampled him and his horse. Afterwards, all they could find were some of his clothes.

Nat Love won a horse raffle when he was 15 years old. He sold the horse and took half the money home to his family. The other half he used to travel to Dodge City, Kansas, to become a cowboy.

Collection of The New-York Historical Society #43431

One July, Nat was in the Dakotas finishing up a delivery of 3,000 cattle. Just 9 days earlier General George Custer and all his soldiers were killed in a fight with Indians at the Little Bighorn. This was an important part of our country's history in the West. They did not know it at the time, but Nat and the other cowboys had been close by herding cattle.

They continued on the road to Deadwood, Dakota Territory. When the cowboys arrived, the whole town was abuzz about the Fourth of July celebrations. Nat decided to enter a roping and shooting contest with a $200 prize.

During his years as a cowboy, Nat shot and killed many buffalo. Once he was caught in the middle of a huge stampede and his friend was trampled to death. They never found his body.

Out of the dozen men participating, 6 of them were free black men. Nat felt right at home in the saddle and quickly lassoed the mustang assigned to him. In 9 minutes flat, he caught him, threw him, and saddled him. Nat had broken the record of the West! He was the instant winner. In the shooting event, he made bull's-eye after bull's-eye and walked away with the prize.

The crowd cheered him on. That day, they changed his name from Red River Dick to Deadwood Dick. "I have always carried the name with honor since that time," said Nat. His roping record was never broken during his career as a cowboy between 1869 and 1890.

In 1877, the first in a series of dime novels was published. It was called *Deadwood Dick: The Prince of the Road or The Black Rider of the Black Hills*. These cheaply printed adventure stories were entertainment for children and adults alike. Although there were over a hundred Deadwood Dick stories, they were not based on any one true person. Many claimed this name, as did Nat Love.

In 1890, Nat decided to call it quits in the cowboy business. He had enjoyed a long, successful career but the times were changing. The coming of the railroad made life different and less exciting for the range riders. He even settled down and married. Still interested in travel and adventure, Nat worked for many years as a Pullman porter for the railroad.

In 1907, Nat decided to write down his adventures. He called his book *The Life and Adventures of Nat Love, better known as "Deadwood Dick" by himself*. The subtitle was *A True History of Slavery Days, Life on the Great Cattle Ranges and the Plains, of the "Wild and Wooly" West, based on facts and personal experiences of the author*.

Nat Love was not the only African-American cowboy. Some went West before and during the war as slaves to help their owners. Some were free blacks who owned their own ranches and slaves. After the Civil War, there were an estimated 5,000 black cowboys who helped tame the wild, Wild West.

In it, Nat describes many adventures and famous people that he met. They included Billy the Kid, Bat Masterson, Buffalo Bill Cody and Jesse James. Like a lot of cowboys, he used exaggeration. His autobiography is very entertaining, but some of the stories seem like tall tales. It is also of interest that in Nat's writings, he did not accept many Indians and Mexicans as equals. This is hard to imagine since he was mistreated himself because of the color of his skin.

Nat Love made his mark in history. His account of the excitement of cowboy life is the only book-length autobiography of an African-American cowboy that we have today. That was quite an accomplishment for a man who used to chase rabbits in his shirttails as a young, uneducated slave.

Nat was enslaved as a young boy, but he went on to become a well-known African-American cowboy—Deadwood Dick. Although he had been mistreated because of the color of his skin, Nat did not have an open-minded attitude about the Mexicans and Indians he met out West. He wrote about this in his book.

Chapter 9

Runaway on the Water
Robert Smalls (1839–1915)

The Secret

"You are in charge, Robert," said Captain C. J. Relyea, stepping off the deck of the *Planter* onto the dock. If he could have read Robert's mind at that moment, he would never have left. But trouble was the last thing he expected from Robert.

Relyea and the other men were looking their best. Their mustaches were waxed, their boots polished, and the brass of their swords and sabers glistened. They were off to a fine party given by the ladies of Charleston. They hoped to dance the night away and forget about the war for a while. If they were lucky, the ladies would find them handsome in their soldier uniforms.

Robert's palms were sweaty as he gripped the steering wheel of the boat, smiled and answered, "Yes, sir." He just knew the captain must smell his fear. He also knew if his plan failed, the punishment could be death. But this was a chance he was more than willing to take.

This night had been planned for a long time and Robert could not believe it was finally here. His heart was thumping with nervous excitement, and every muscle in his body was tense. So far, everything was going just as he had planned.

The soldiers had made it so easy, just as he had hoped. He could not believe that Captain Relyea could be so stupid and careless. The rule was the captain or one of his men must remain on board ship at all times. With the laughter and fun on their minds, Relyea and the crew slipped ashore trusting Robert to be in charge.

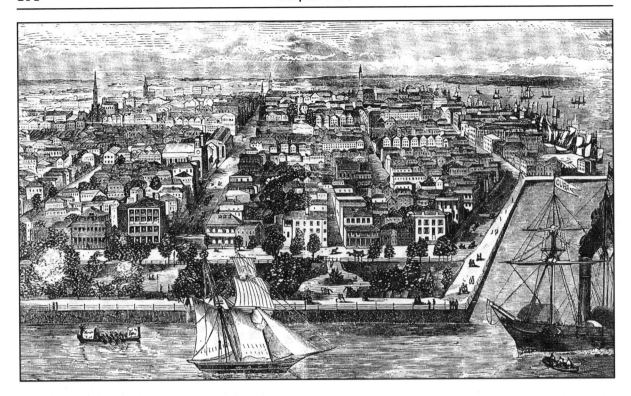

Charleston, South Carolina, was a busy port. This is where Robert's theft of the **Planter** *began.*

Little did these soldiers know that the race for freedom was just beginning for this brave band of enslaved people—and danger was around the corner for the Confederate soldiers. Robert had been wheelman of the steamboat for over a year now. It was originally used to haul cotton by owner John Ferguson. Like many men loyal to the Confederacy, he let the government use his boat to run supplies for the troops along the rivers and creeks of coastal South Carolina. His paddlewheeler was large enough to carry 1,000 men or 1,400 bales of cotton. Plus, it could run in shallow waters where other boats ran aground.

Robert was a very skilled wheelman for a 23-year-old. He also was smart and remembered where all the torpedoes were buried in the harbor. It was important to navigate around them. Robert was also brave. He had been a slave long enough, and he was willing to risk his life.

For many months, he had been saving to buy his wife and children's freedom—$800 was the price his owner wanted. It made him angry every time he thought about another man owning his family. If the conditions were right, he would show the world what a black man could do. He planned to steal the *Planter* right from under the noses of the soldiers at Fort Sumter. It would mean a 7-mile run to the Union ships and freedom.

The **Planter** *was quite a catch for the Union navy. She could travel in shallow waters where other boats hit the bottom. Her pilot, Robert Smalls, knew where all the Confederate torpedoes were buried.*

Harper's Weekly

Soon, it was after midnight and the soldiers were ashore in an exhausted sleep from their night of partying. Robert and the other men found the captain's guns and one of his uniforms. It was in the early hours of May 13, 1862, and the *Planter* was on its way.

The first stop was the dock of the *Etowan*. Robert's wife, Hannah, and their two children, Elizabeth, and Robert Jr., were hiding there with the other wives and children. Besides the 5 women and 3 children on the *Planter*, there were 9 men on board: Robert Smalls and his brother, John, Alfred Gridiron, William Morrison, J. Chisholm, A. Alston, Gabriel Turno, and Abraham Jackson. The steward of the *Etowan* decided to come at the last minute.

Robert's palms grew even sweatier. Now, he would have to put his plan to the test. He eased the *Planter* out into the harbor. As he passed first Castle Pinckney and then Fort Johnson, Robert gave the expected steam whistle salutes. He held his breath, but the sentry just waved him by as usual. His good luck held as he sailed past Fort Moultrie.

Now for the biggest obstacle of all: Fort Sumter. If they could make it past this point, they were safe. Robert was very fearful as the night faded and the first rays of sunlight crept across the water. What if he was recognized? Those powerful Sumter cannons would blow him out of the water. But he played his part well, wearing the hat of the captain and acting as if it were business as usual.

Fort Sumter was where the Civil War began. Here citizens of Charleston watch the firing on the fort. Robert Smalls fooled the guards at Fort Sumter and piloted a stolen boat right past them.

Frank Leslie's *Our Soldier in the Civil War*

When the *Planter* took a different turn, the guard at Fort Sumter was puzzled. As the steamship suddenly picked up speed, he knew he had made a terrible mistake letting it pass. He desperately sent signals to shore. By now the runaway ship was too far out to sea to catch it.

The next stop was the USS *Onward,* the first ship in the front of the Union fleet. The fugitive slaves lowered the Rebel flag and hoisted the white flag of truce. The crew of the *Onward* did not know what to make of this Rebel ship in enemy waters and readied their guns. What if this was a trick?

Imagine their surprise when the *Planter* pulled up alongside their ship with a group of cheering black men, women, and children. Their fearless leader, Robert Smalls, announced they were returning "some of your old U.S. guns, sir."

The reaction to the theft of the *Planter* was strong. Citizens were just furious that a mere slave had stolen a paddlewheel steamer at daybreak. Some thought slaves were not smart enough to do such a thing. The soldiers who left their posts were tried, fined, and put in prison. One Virginia newspaper said that these soldiers should be put in "petticoats or straitjackets for the rest of the war."

The newspapers of **Charleston, South Carolina,** printed stories on May 14, 1862. It reported that citizens were "intensely agitated" about the news that the *Planter* was taken over "by her colored crew." At first, they refused to believe it.

Overnight Hero

In the North, Robert Smalls instantly became famous. Newspapers far and wide covered the story of his escapade, calling it "one of the most daring and heroic adventures" of the war. His photograph appeared in publications. Even in France, the newspapers printed stories about Robert and his amazing escape.

It was the custom at the time for people to receive the price of captured ships and guns as a reward. Congress passed a resolution to do this for Robert and his crew. Secretary of the Navy Gideon Welles valued the boat and the guns at $9,168 even though similar boats were several times this amount. Because the heroes were enslaved black men, they received only half the value of the boat.

For his heroic deed, Robert received $1,500, and his crew got about $400 apiece. This was a lot of money, but it angered the *Planter*'s crew that they did not get the same amount white men would. To top it all off, the Congress put their money into savings accounts and gave them a little bit each year.

It took a while for all the excitement to sink in for the Union leaders. At first, they did not realize what a prize they had. Not only did they have a captured ship; they also had Robert Smalls. He could show them all the torpedoes the Confederate

These brave, black men captured the Planter and turned her over to the Union navy. There were 9 male slaves on board when they stole the steamer.

Frank Leslie's *Our Soldier in the Civil War*

Robert was only 23 years old when he stole the Planter. The people of Charleston were horrified that a black man had fooled the soldiers at Fort Sumter.

Harper's Weekly

Gideon Welles, secretary of the navy, recommended that Robert and his crew receive rewards for capturing the* Planter. *Because they were black, they only received half the amount due them.

soldiers had set, plus he knew the best water routes. Having heard many of the Confederate officers discussing plans, Robert was like their very own spy!

In addition, on board the *Planter* were 4 guns. Robert also knew there were no guns left on Cole Island, since he and his crew had moved them to Fort Ripley. Now, the Union not only had the 4 additional guns, but they knew that Cole Island was unarmed and abandoned. This left Charleston easy to attack.

Robert urged the Union forces to move in at once. They did a scouting mission but dragged their feet for close to 8 weeks before bringing in troops. This meant they lost the opportunity to capture Charleston early in the war. In a brutal fight, they lost 600 of their men on James Island. Robert knew this would never have happened if they had listened to him.

Until now, President Lincoln and other leaders were not sure they wanted black men serving as soldiers. However, General David Hunter, in charge of the War Department in the South, had big ideas about using escaped slaves as soldiers. He even organized the first black regiment, the 1st South Carolina Volunteers, without permission. He had no money, guns, or food for his soldiers. Hunter was fearful he would have to send them all home soon without Lincoln's support.

Generals David Hunter and Rufus Saxton put their heads together and decided to use Robert Smalls as a secret weapon. They sent him to Washington to meet with Secretary of War Edwin Stanton. If the men in charge met Robert and heard about his amazing capture of the *Planter,* maybe they would see what black soldiers could do. Whatever Robert said must have worked. He came home with orders for Saxton to organize up to 5,000 black soldiers.

Next, Saxton and Hunter sent Robert and his family up North for a speaking tour. For several weeks, he appeared at churches and civic halls to tell the story of his daring escape. One group of women promised to make a regimental flag for the 1st South Carolina Volunteers. Other people gave money for food and to help teachers educate the freed people on the coastal islands.

> By the time the Civil War ended, **200,000 blacks** served in the Union army and navy. Robert Smalls helped convince Washington leaders that blacks had a contribution to make in the war effort.

Although blacks wanted to serve in the army, they were given manual labor jobs during the war. President Lincoln eventually let them serve as soldiers. Many, like the 54th Massachusetts, were well known for their bravery.

Frank Leslie's *Our Soldier in the Civil War*

At one appearance at Shiloh Church in New York, Robert was greeted with wild cheers and a standing ovation. Here he received an award from the black community. The engraving read: "Presented to Robert Smalls by the Colored Citizens of New York, October 2, 1862, as a token of their regard for his heroism, his love of liberty and his patriotism."

Robert may have been loved in the North, but in the South it was a different story. In November, soon after his trip north, Robert and his family learned there were black men in his neighborhood who were sent to kidnap him. There was a $4,000 reward offered in Charleston for his capture! Fortunately, these men were discovered before they could catch up with Robert.

Military Service

Realizing what a good ship pilot he was, the army put Robert on the payroll for $50 a month. Here, there was little chance of him being caught with Union soldiers all around. Although Robert was in 17 war skirmishes, there were 2 that were especially exciting.

In April 1863, Admiral Samuel Du Pont decided to take back Fort Sumter. His bold plan was to use all the ironclad ships to attack. The smallest ship of all was the USS *Keokuk,* and its pilot would be Robert Smalls.

As the fleet of ships sailed towards the fort, the 300 guns of Fort Sumter fired away. The captain asked Robert to sail in front of the other ships straight for the fort. For 30 minutes, Robert met the enemy head-on. Bullets were flying all around him and he was frightened. But he held steady. His ironside was peppered with holes. The *Keokuk* took 90 hits in all and had to retreat. The rest of the fleet followed shortly behind.

> Robert Smalls became a navy pilot at an important time in our country's naval history. **The first navy battle** between ironclad ships took place during the Civil War. The two ironclads were the USS *Monitor* and the CSS *Virginia.* (CSS *Virginia* was originally the USS *Merrimack.*)

Later that night, the *Keokuk* sank much to Robert's dismay. Although the battle was not a success, Robert proved the black man's bravery in the line of fire.

About 6 months later, Robert was again piloting the *Planter* near Secessionville, South Carolina. Suddenly, their boat was under fierce attack. Captain Nickerson panicked and ordered Robert to beach the boat and surrender. After all he had been through on this ship, Robert was not about to turn it over to the Rebels. As the frightened captain ran and hid under the coal bin, Robert ignored his orders. He got the crew on his side and they battled their way out to safety.

When they reached the shore, Robert was terrified. He thought he had done the right thing, but disobeying orders could cost him his pilot's position. Instead he was pleasantly surprised. The commanding officers dismissed Nickerson as a coward and named Robert as captain in his place. Never before had a black man been made captain of a ship in the United States! Not only that, but he received a message that same day that he was a father again. He had a new baby girl, Sarah. The news lightened his heavy heart—his son, Robert Jr., had died earlier that year from smallpox.

> Twenty-five of every 100 men in the **U.S. Navy** were black men. Some were ex-slaves, and some were free blacks.

In the meantime, the *Planter* was slowly wearing out, falling apart piece by piece. The navy decided the ship was too important to give up, so they sent Robert to Philadelphia for its repairs. While there, he visited the shipyard to watch the work.

*The **Planter** was a steamer like the boats pictured here. She transported soldiers and guns for the Confederacy until Robert stole her right out of Charleston harbor.*

Frank Leslie's *Our Soldier in the Civil War*

One day, Robert took a streetcar back to his room. He got aboard and paid for his ticket. The conductor told Robert that he had to go outside on the platform. Robert wanted to know why, and was told it was a company rule that blacks could not ride in the cars.

At first, Robert refused to go outside, and then he asked the conductor to stop the car. He announced he would leave rather than ride on the platform. The Philadelphia newspapers found out that a famous war hero was denied a seat, and it was big news. Soon many white people were refusing to ride the streetcars. There were even large public meetings held to protest the rule. As a result, some companies changed their policies. Two years after the war ended, the state leaders passed a law that ended this practice.

Once the *Planter* was back in the South, Robert became a pilot again. Not long after that, the Rebels gave up Charleston, and Robert returned to the city as a hero. In April 1865, he was heading the famous boat for Fort Sumter with 3,000 freedmen on board for a flag-raising ceremony of the Stars and Stripes. It was a highly emotional day for Robert and his people.

Their happiness was soon spoiled by terrible news. President Lincoln was invited to the flag ceremony. Instead he went to the Ford's Theatre where he was shot and killed by John Wilkes Booth. People across the country were shocked and saddened, especially the former slaves.

Congressman Smalls

In the days after the war known as Reconstruction, efforts were made to rebuild the war-torn South. Robert and other freedmen learned some hard lessons. Many of the freedoms they had fought for did not come so easily. General William Tecumseh Sherman had promised the sea island freedmen 40 acres apiece to start their new lives. But Congress began to take pity on the former plantation owners and took back this promise along with the land. When General Saxton protested, they moved him into a job up North.

Just when things were looking bad, Robert had some good luck. In March of 1863, the house of his former owner, Henry McKee, was put up for sale at a government auction. Robert was born in the slave quarters of this house years ago and he decided to put in a bid of $600. To his surprise, he became the new owner of this lovely Beaufort, South Carolina, home. One of his first projects in his new neighborhood was to start a school for the black children.

In the first years after the war, the Southern states were asked to write new constitutions. In South Carolina, the new lawmakers wrote a black code of conduct. The black community could not believe the rules. The only jobs they could hold were farmer or hired servant. White men could fire them when they wanted and even whip them. No black man could testify against a white man in court. Robert and his family thought the war accomplished nothing.

The white men did everything they could to frighten black voters in that first state election. But the black community in

> "There are now men in congress who are willing to vote...to have us sent out of the country. These men forget that the negroes of the country gave 186,000 men who fought in two hundred and fifty-two battles for the perpetuity of this great nation. We do not intend to go anywhere, but will remain right here and help make this the most powerful of all governments." —Robert Smalls

After the war, Robert Smalls served in the South Carolina House of Representatives, and also served in the U.S. Congress.

Library of Congress

Beaufort stood strong and elected Robert to represent them. The first thing the new state legislature did was vote to write another state constitution. The black code was taken out.

There were more hard times to come for the black people of South Carolina. In 1875, just as Robert Smalls was elected to the U.S. Congress, another group was forming. They called themselves the "Red Shirts."

This group soon put their military drills in action. The small town of Hamburg, South Carolina, was about to become the site of a massacre. Forty black men were practicing their own military drills when they were suddenly attacked by 2,000 Red Shirts. Many of them were murdered in cold blood. The black community was in terror as they watched their homes and businesses burning. Robert Smalls made sure the Washington newspapers heard about the tragedy. He even got the government to send troops to make sure the governor's election was fair.

The Red Shirts was a group of former Confederate soldiers who organized in South Carolina to terrorize blacks and to prevent their participation in government. The color of red symbolized blood, and the Red Shirts did not hesitate to shed blood to achieve their goals. The group met regularly to practice military drills.

The Red Shirts tried every trick they knew to keep the black people from voting. When this did not work, they cheated. Benjamin Tillman, who later served as governor, was quoted as saying, "We stuffed ballot boxes; we shot Negroes; we are not ashamed of it." In one county, there were 2,200 more votes than voters. In the end, both sides claimed they won. One governor ruled in the state house, the other ruled in the state senate.

A **lynching** is the illegal hanging of a person without a trial. People often took the law into their own hands in the period following the Civil War. Often, black people were the victims.

Through all the hard times, Robert continued to be a leader of his people. He encouraged them to be brave and to stand up for their rights. One of his last acts of bravery occurred in Beaufort. It was a brutal custom of the time for white people to take the law into their own hands, and Robert had to step in.

This soldier was hanged for his crime. After the Civil War, many innocent black people were hanged without trials. This was known as lynching. In Beaufort, South Carolina, Robert Smalls prevented a lynching by threatening to burn buildings and homes.

Library of Congress, Photograph by Mathew Brady

On one occasion, a white mob was threatening to lynch two accused black men. Robert and the black community were determined to keep that from happening. They came up with a plan and told the sheriff about it. Throughout the city, they stood ready to light fires in the white neighborhoods if the white mob hanged those men.

The sheriff quickly guarded the roads into town. He knew that Robert meant what he said. There was no doubt in his mind that those homes would be burned. For two days, everyone was frightened. Would the mob get through? Would Beaufort burn? Finally, the sheriff talked down the angry whites and the lynching was prevented. Robert's leadership had worked once again.

Sadly, Robert developed many enemies over the years. They succeeded in having false bribery charges brought against him. Next, they tried to drive him out of Washington. When he started his term in Congress, there were 8 black men

serving. Over the years, the white men worked to vote them out of office. Finally, there was just Robert and one other black man left. Robert lost his seat in a crooked election in 1886. He asked Congress to investigate. By a close congressional vote of 142 to 127, he lost his seat.

Robert Smalls will be remembered as a black leader for many reasons. He was among the bravest of runaway slaves, risking death in his capture of the *Planter*. He proved himself in the line of fire and was made an officer in the Union navy.

This photograph shows Robert Smalls around 1895. He was a leader all his life in the armed forces, the South Carolina legislature, and the U.S. Congress.
Courtesy of South Carolina Library, University of South Carolina

This engraving shows Port Royal harbor. During Robert's career as a U.S. congressman, he persuaded Congress to put a naval station here. Today, it is called Parris Island, the training grounds for the U.S. Marines.
Frank Leslie's *Our Soldier in the Civil War*

He was an elected state and national official and a leader in the Republican Party. He defended his people during the violence of the postwar years.

Robert was proud of his service as a U.S. congressman. One of his accomplishments that is well remembered across the U.S. was the placing of a naval station at Port Royal, South Carolina. The young 23-year-old slave who captured the *Planter* became the man to bring the future training grounds for the U.S. Marine Corps to his native state. Today, we know it as Parris Island.

———————————————

If you visit Charleston, South Carolina, be sure to stop at Fort Moultrie, the fort that Robert Smalls sailed past when he stole the Planter. *The National Park Service operates a site there. If you call ahead, 843-883-3123, you can arrange to view videos on Robert Smalls and the famous 54th Massachusetts Infantry.*

Chapter 10

A Woman of Truth
Sojourner Truth (1797–1883)

Isabella Hardenburgh was only 9 years old, but she had the worries of a grown-up woman. All around her were frightening sounds. The group of men laughing and slapping each other on the back made her tremble. As far as they were concerned, this was a social occasion. For a young slave girl, it was not. The auctioneer's loud voice rang in her ears, reminding her why she was there.

She suspected for a long time that this day might come, but she had always hoped it would not. So young and frightened, she did not know what would happen to her now. All she knew was the auctioneer would be calling for her any minute. Once she was sold, she might never again see the farm in Ulster County, New York, where she grew up.

Standing there shaking with fright, she remembered the story that Mau-mau and Baumfree, her parents, had told her about her older brother and sister. One winter morning when a white, fluffy snow carpeted the ground, her brother, Michael, was promised a sleigh ride. He was excited until he saw a white man take their sister, Nancy, out of their cabin and lock her into the sleigh box.

Hearing his sister's screams, he suddenly realized what was happening. Mr. Hardenburgh, their owner, had sold them without a word of warning to anyone. The children wept for their parents as the sleigh quickly glided down the road and out of sight of their childhood home. Isabella's family never heard from Michael and Nancy again.

When Mau-mau grew too sad thinking of her lost children, she often looked up into the night sky. She told her young daughter that God was always watching over them and that she could talk to him anytime she was in trouble. He lived in the sky, she said, pointing toward the heavens.

> Those are the same stars, and that is the same moon, that look down upon your brothers and sisters and which they see as they look up at them, though they are ever so far away from us and each other.

Isabella knew that soon she would be looking at those evening stars for comfort when she thought of her family. For now, she had to endure the embarrassment of being put on the auction block in front of everyone. Here, any interested buyer could poke and prod, examining her body or her teeth, all he wanted.

Suddenly, it was all over. Mr. John Neely had paid $100 for Isabella and the herd of sheep that went with her. She did not know it at the time, but she would only see her parents 3 more times before they died. Baumfree would be abandoned.

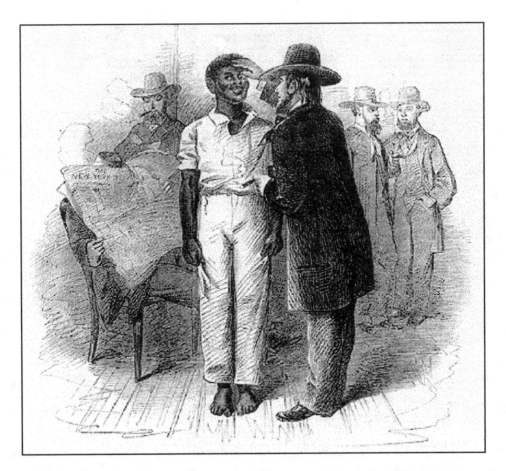

Sojourner was 9 years old when she was first sold. It was a common practice for buyers to examine slaves as shown in this old engraving.

Harper's Weekly

He then starved to death after Mau-mau died of a sudden illness, leaving him help-less and alone.

Life at the Neelys was so hard. For one thing, Mau-mau and Baumfree had never taught Isabella to speak English. There was no need to because her first owner was Dutch. The Neelys grew more and more impatient with her since she did not understand any of the orders they gave her.

Isabella's owners finally decided she was just being stubborn. Mr. Neely thought she needed a lesson in obedience. One morning Isabella was called to the barn where her owner had heated metal rods in the embers. Years later, she told a friend what happened next:

> When he had tied her hands together before her, he gave her the most cruel whipping she was ever tortured with. He whipped her til the flesh was deeply lacerated, and the blood streamed from her wounds—and the scars remain to the present day, to testify to the fact. "And now," she says, "when I hear 'em tell of whipping women on the bare flesh, it makes my flesh crawl, and my very hair rise on my head! Oh! My God!...what a way is this of treating human beings?"

After 2 miserable years with the Neelys, Isabella was sold again to Martin Schryver for $105. Mr. Schryver was a fisherman and an innkeeper, and a much gentler owner than Mr. Neely. Isabella worked very hard fishing and hoeing corn for her new owners, but she never had to worry about any more terrible beatings. At long last, she learned to speak English. Nonetheless, she was just a slave to the Schryvers, and her life with them lasted only a year and a half. When they had an opportunity to sell her for $300, they could not resist the money.

John Dumont was the man who paid such a big price for Isabella, and he ex-pected a lot of work from her. Mau-mau had always taught her to say her prayers, mind her owner, and to never lie or steal. Isabella knew she would try her best to get along with Mr. Dumont. His wife was another story.

Belle, as the Dumonts came to call her, got into trouble almost immediately. No matter what she did, the breakfast potatoes were always black. Mrs. Dumont thought Belle was not washing them, and she repeatedly punished her for the dirty potatoes.

For some reason, the white kitchen girl named Kate, who worked with Belle, did not like her. The Dumont's daughter, Gertrude, finally solved the mystery of the black potatoes. She caught Kate throwing ashes into the potato pot just to get Belle in trouble. Soon things became better between Belle and her mistress.

Belle was just a young teenager when she came to the Dumont family, but she was their property for close to 17 years. In her early years there, like many young

These field hands labored from sunup to sundown. Sojourner worked long hours in the cornfields when Mr. Schryver owned her.

Picking cotton was backbreaking work. Children not old enough to work went to the fields with their mothers.

girls, she fell in love. Unfortunately, Robert lived on the nearby Caitlin plantation. One day when Robert was sneaking over for a visit with Belle, Mr. Caitlin and his two sons came and found him. They were very angry and viciously beat him with heavy wooden sticks. Mr. Dumont stopped them before they beat Robert to death.

Belle's heart was broken. Robert was afraid to disobey his owner again, so he married a woman on his own plantation as Mr. Caitlin wished. When Mr. Dumont picked an older slave named Thomas to marry Belle, she did not argue. If she could not have the man she loved, she would accept her owner's orders. She and Thomas had 5 children together: Diana, Peter, Elizabeth, and Sophia. Another one of their babies, Hannah, died.

Although many slaves lived in the South, some like Belle grew up in the North where laws were sometimes different. In 1817, a New York law passed giving slaves freedom in 10 years. Belle looked forward to that time. She worked harder than ever to please her owner. Dumont even agreed to free her one-year early if she would continue working so hard.

Unfortunately, Belle hurt her hand that year. When she went to Mr. Dumont on the day she expected her freedom, he told her she would have to work one more year. He said she had not done as much work as usual because of her injury.

Belle was so angry! She had pushed herself hard all year long, looking forward to her freedom. The other slaves had warned her not to trust the promise of a white man, but she did not listen. Because her owner had double-crossed her, she made a decision to run away.

Heartbroken at leaving her children behind with their father, Belle sneaked away from the Dumont farm before dawn one morning. Baby Sophia was in her arms. For a while she was frightened and did not know where to go. A neighbor told her of a Quaker couple named Isaac and Maria Van Wagener, known for opposing slavery.

After hearing her sad story, the Van Wageners agreed to hire her. These were the first white people Belle ever met who asked her to call them by their first names.

Mr. Dumont was most upset when he found Belle was missing. She was a valuable piece of property and he did not mean to give her up. He went to the Van Wagener home demanding her return.

> A **Quaker** is a person who is a member of the Society of Friends, the name of a religious organization. During the years prior to the Civil War, Quakers were active in the anti-slavery movement and the Underground Railroad. Quakers were often involved in peace and equality issues.

When Belle heard his orders, she announced she would never go back and would never give up her baby, Sophia. Isaac Van Wagener stepped in and offered to buy Belle's services for the rest of the year for $20 and an extra $5 for Sophia. Still disturbed by the loss of his hardest worker, Dumont had little choice but to agree. But within a short while, he was ruining Belle's life again.

Belle received word that her son, Peter, had been sold. Why did Dumont continue to torture her so? Peter's new owner then decided to sell him to a planter in Alabama. Belle was not only a hard-working person; she was also very intelligent. She knew it was against the law in New York to sell a slave out of the state.

As fast as she could get there, Belle was at the Dumont property complaining about the illegal sale. Mrs. Dumont scolded her saying what "a fine fuss to make about a little" black baby. (But she used a word that many slave owners used at that time.) With great strength and courage, Belle answered her in a deep, solemn voice: "I will have my child again." Anyone hearing the tone of her voice knew she meant what she said.

Somehow Belle overcame her fears and did what no slave dared do before. She went to the nearest courthouse to ask for help. Slaves, especially females, had few or no legal rights. That did not stop Belle. This was unheard of, but she did not care. She did not know it at the time, but she was making history. It took many miles of walking to deliver papers and to raise money for the lawyer, but it worked.

When the court officials finally saw that she was honest and that the law was broken, they gave her the papers to get her son back. Belle became the first black person at that time to ever win a court case against a white man. Peter was now back in his mother's care. But Belle was shocked and angry when she examined her young son. He had cuts and scars all over his body from his cruel owner. Some months later, Belle learned that this owner had attacked and murdered his wife. She shuddered to think what might have happened to her son.

All her life, Belle had been a religious woman. Her mother had taught her to look to God for help in times of trouble. Belle talked to God every day and had very intense religious experiences and visions during her prayers. She said she could feel "It was God all around me." When she first discovered Jesus, she says she "began to feel such a love in my soul as I never felt before—love to all creatures."

At this point in her life, religion became the most important thing for Belle. In 1829, she moved to New York City and became involved with churches and religious groups. She went to the big city with Peter and Sophia, hoping God would lead them to better jobs and a better life. Free blacks had to earn their own living, and she was finding it more and more difficult to care for her family.

While working for New York families, she met a religious leader, Elijah Pierson. Elijah formed an unusual religious community called The Kingdom, and Belle went to live there. She followed all of Elijah's teachings, including fasting. Poor Belle worked day and night for the kingdom, doing all the cooking and cleaning. She wanted so badly to be involved in work to serve God. She even gave the kingdom her hard-earned money.

Before long, another man named Robert Matthews joined the group. He changed his name to Matthias and soon he and Elijah were in competition to be leaders. The Kingdom began to get stranger and stranger in its religious practices. Matthias started admiring other men's wives and wanted the members to bathe together as a group. Then, Elijah Pierson died very suddenly for no reason and Matthias was arrested under suspicion of murder.

> **Fasting** means going without food for hours or days. Some religious groups practice fasting to show their devotion and to strengthen the discipline of their beliefs.

Imagine poor Belle's terrible shock when one of the kingdom families, the Folgers, accused her of poisoning Elijah and their family! Some people even called her a witch. All of this after she had worked so hard for them. She was even accused in the newspapers.

Having been successful once before, Belle went to court again. She found a good lawyer and sued the family who made up these terrible lies. The judge made the Folgers pay Belle $125. She also became the friend of a writer named Gilbert Hale, who helped her tell her story and clear her good name.

When the kingdom failed, it was a terrible disappointment for Belle. She began to feel very unhappy and dissatisfied with her life. One day in 1843, she could stand it no longer. She went to Mrs. Whiting, her employer, and told her she was leaving. An hour later she had packed her things and was out the door. "The Spirit calls me...and I must go," she said.

Belle was a person with very strong feelings and opinions. It was very important to her to do work that would help other people and to preach about the wrongs in the world. She knew in her heart that slavery was a terrible sin against the human race. She felt that God had called her to travel all across the country, preaching and teaching and singing. Somehow Belle did not seem like a name for a preacher and teacher. She needed a new name for her new job. She said:

> I went to the Lord and asked him to give me a new name. And the Lord gave me Sojourner, because I was to travel up and down the land, showing the people their sins, and being a sign unto them.

God was a symbol of truth for her, so she took that as her last name. In the past, her last name was the same as her owner. God was her new owner now. Soon, Sojourner Truth would be known across America for her powerful speaking and preaching.

People sat up and paid attention when Sojourner talked. Nearly 6 feet tall, she made quite an impression. She always wore a long black or grey dress with a white shawl and a white head covering. Having a good sense of humor, she kept people interested in what she said. Posters advertised her free speeches and everywhere she went, people lined up to hear this black woman preacher, who they heard so much about.

She never learned to read and write, but Sojourner knew her Bible inside and out. On the subject of slavery, she became a fiery speaker. Not only was she hoping to see the slaves freed; she wanted to keep the slave owners from going to hell for their sins.

Sojourner was a brave woman. She was never afraid to stand up and say what she thought. Once at a camp meeting, a group of angry young men came to stir up trouble. The people in charge asked them to leave, but the men became even more determined to disrupt the event. Sojourner should have been terrified, especially since she was the only black person there.

> At one of Sojourner Truth's speeches, a man in the audience angrily told her that he cared no more about her talk on slavery than the bite of a flea.
>
> Sojourner answered him, **"Perhaps, not, but the Lord willing, I'll keep you scratching."**

Instead she proudly marched to the top of a nearby hill and began singing in a loud voice. This grabbed the attention of the boys who came to hear what she had to say. She told them she was not hurting anyone and asked why they carried sticks and clubs. The young men grew quiet and listened to her talking and singing. Soon, they quietly made their way home. Over the years, Sojourner was able to quiet many angry crowds.

But the speech for which Sojourner became most famous was made in Akron, Ohio, at a women's convention in 1851. She sat quietly listening to speakers for a couple of days. When several ministers rose to speak against women's rights, she could be silent no longer. They said women were weaker, and men were smarter and stronger. As proof, they said that Jesus was a man. Belle had heard enough.

The crowd grew suddenly quiet as Sojourner marched up front to speak. She reminded the ministers that a man had

Sojourner Truth walked hundreds of miles to spread the word that slavery was evil.

Library of Congress

nothing to do with the birth of Jesus. After all, he came from God and his mother, Mary. Then she spoke these words that people would remember for years and years to come:

> Well, children, where there is so much racket there must be something out of kilter. I think that 'twixt the negroes of the South and the women at the North, all talking about rights, the white men will be in a fix pretty soon. But what's all this here talking about? That man over there says that women need to be helped into carriages, and lifted over ditches and to have the best place everywhere. Nobody ever helps me into carriages, or over mud-puddles, or gives me any best place. And ain't I a woman?

At this point in her speech, Sojourner rolled up her sleeve to show her strong, muscled arm:

> Look at me! Look at my arm! I have ploughed and planted, and gathered into barns, and no man could head me! And ain't I a woman? I could work as much and eat as much as a man—when I could get it—and bear the lash as well! And ain't I a woman? I have born...children and seen most all sold off

Solving a History Mystery: What did Sojourner really say?

Today there is a controversy, or debate, about Sojourner Truth's speech at the Women's Rights Convention. Some historians are convinced that Sojourner Truth never said, "Ain't I a woman?" They say these words were recorded 12 years later by Convention Chairwoman Frances Gage when she was writing a newspaper article.

These historians believe the more correct version of Sojourner's speech is the one written by a newspaper reporter who was there at the time—Mr. Marius Robinson from the *Anti-Slavery Bugle* whose story was published nearly a month later on June 21, 1851.

In his account, Sojourner said: "I am a woman's rights. I have as much muscle as any man, and can do as much work as any man. I have plowed and reaped and husked and chopped and mowed, and can any man do more than that?...

"I have heard much about the sexes being equal; I can carry as much as any man, and can eat as much as one too, if I can get it. I am as strong as any man that is now. As for intellect, all I can say is, if woman have a pint and man a quart—why can't she have her little pint full?

"And how came Jesus into this world? Through God who created him and woman who bore him. Man, where is your part?...But man is in a tight place, the poor slave is on him, woman is coming on him and he is surely between a hawk and a buzzard."

Other historians strongly insist that Sojourner did say, "Ain't I a woman?" What do you think? Which speech did Sojourner make? Only she knows for sure, and she took this secret with her on November 26, 1883, the date of her death. Whichever speech Sojourner made, she worked hard all her life for justice and equality for all people.

to slavery, and when I cried out a mother's grief, none but Jesus heard me! And ain't I a woman?

The crowd, the men included, listened with respect to her strong and powerful words. Some applauded and some sat in silence, but there was no doubt that Sojourner had captured everyone's attention.

Over the years, Sojourner traveled throughout the country carrying her message of equality for all people. She visited 22 states in all, walking much of the time. In her lifetime, she covered thousands of miles and preached to hundreds of people. Often the people in her audience were white, and she was able to persuade many of them that slavery was wrong.

One of Sojourner's friends, Olive Gilbert, wanted more people to hear her message. She encouraged her to publish a book, but Sojourner still could not read or write. So Olive listened to Sojourner tell her life story, and she wrote it down for her. *The Narrative of Sojourner Truth* was published in 1850 and is still for sale today.

James Cadwell, the grandson of Sojourner Truth, served in the all-black 54th Massachusetts Infantry. James was captured in South Carolina and was not released until 1865.

About this time, Sojourner also started what she called *The Book of Life.* In it, she wrote stories, experiences, and letters about her travels. She also collected signatures from many famous people such as Harriet Beecher Stowe, William Lloyd Garrison, Susan B. Anthony, and abolitionists Lydia and Lucretia Mott.

Of course when the Civil War started, Sojourner Truth could not sit in silence. She had to be involved. She held a Thanksgiving dinner for black soldiers in Michigan with food donated by nearby neighbors. She stayed to speak and entertain the men, and even led them in singing. Except she changed the words to a familiar tune: "We can shoot a rebel farther than a white man ever saw, As we go marching on."

In 1864, Sojourner was almost 70 years old when she decided she must visit President Lincoln. She left Michigan that spring for Washington, D.C.

Susan B. Anthony worked for the vote for women. She signed the Book of Life, *a book Sojourner carried on all her travels. Many famous people such as President Lincoln and William Lloyd Garrison signed it.*
Library of Congress

(Left) *Sojourner Truth and Abraham Lincoln look at the Bible presented by black citizens of Baltimore in 1864.*

(Below) *When Sojourner boarded a streetcar in Washington, a conductor tried to throw her off and dislocated her shoulder. She took her case to court and won. He lost his job.*

Here freedmen are receiving food rations.

Many blacks were forced to live in refugee camps once they were free. Sojourner worked for the Freedmen's Relief Association and assisted refugees. She protected them from slave hunters coming into camp.

It took her until September to get there, but she got an appointment with the president, whom she wished "to advise." At the end of their talk, he signed her book: "For Aunty Sojourner Truth, A. Lincoln, Oct. 29, 1864."

Sojourner decided to stay in Washington to see how she could help. Many freed slaves had come to live there but they had no jobs and no homes. Hundreds of homeless blacks were living in refugee camps. Many were dying of starvation, sickness, and exposure to the bad weather. Sojourner was appointed as a counselor for the National Freedmen's Relief Association. She found food, shelter, and legal advice for as many suffering people as she could.

One day, Sojourner tried to get onto a Washington streetcar. She was so tired from working hard all day. She was feeling proud that she had been appointed to the Freedmen's Hospital and was put in charge of managing the care of black patients. This was quite an honor for a black woman to be named to such a position.

> **Problems in Camp**
>
> During 1864–65, slave traders were coming into the refugee camps to kidnap free blacks to sell down South. They also bribed the guards to ignore what they were doing.
>
> Sojourner resisted their efforts every way she could, and advised the former slaves of their legal rights. When the camp guards threatened to arrest her, Sojourner said, **"If you put me in the guard house, I will make the United States rock like a cradle."**

So she found it insulting when the streetcar driver did not want to stop for her to ride. She made enough noise to finally get it to stop, only to be told to sit in the black section, or she would be thrown off. Sojourner kept her seat and refused to move. Gaining equality on the streetcars became her next project.

On another occasion, when the conductor tried to remove her, he dislocated her shoulder. Once again, Sojourner turned to the courts. She sued the conductor for attacking her. Not only did the conductor lose his case, he was fired. The companies had to change their policies as well.

Never one to sit by when there was a wrong to right, Sojourner became a legend of her time. In her 86 years of life, she always had courage. She was the only black woman of her time to win three court battles. With the power of her words, this former slave who never learned to read or write changed people's hearts and helped bring an end to the institution of slavery.

———————

One thousand people attended the funeral of Sojourner Truth on November 26, 1883. The temporary marker on her grave fell apart over time, and her story quietly faded into the past. In 1915, the city of Battle Creek, Michigan, even razed her home in a cleanup campaign. In 1961, a permanent historical marker was placed on her grave. On July 4, 1997, the National Aeronautics and Space Administration (NASA) launched a mission to Mars. The name of the robotic space rover was the Sojourner Truth.

Suggested Reading

Adler, David A. *A Picture Book of Sojourner Truth.* Illustrated by Gershom Griffith. New York: Holiday House, 1994.

Cavanah, Frances. *The Truth About the Man Behind the Book That Sparked the War Between the States.* Philadelphia: Westminster Press, 1975.

Felton, Harold W. *Nat Love: Negro Cowboy.* New York: Dodd, Mead & Company, 1969.

Graham, Shirley. *Booker T. Washington: Educator of Hand, Head, and Heart.* New York: Julian Messner, 1955.

Hakim, Joy. *History of Us: War, Terrible War 1860–1865.* Book 6. New York: Oxford University Press, 1999.

Jordan, Denise. *Susie King Taylor: Destined to be Free.* Illustrated by Higgins Bond. Orange, N.J.: Just Us Books, 1994.

Krass, Peter. *Sojourner Truth: Antislavery Activist.* New York: Chelsea House, 1988.

Lester, Julius. *To Be a Slave.* New York: Scholastic, Inc., 1968.

Lyons, Mary. *Letters from a Slave Girl: The Story of Harriet Jacobs.* New York: Aladdin Paperbacks, 1996.

Ortiz, Victoria. *Sojourner Truth: A Self-Made Woman.* Philadelphia: J. B. Lippincott Company, 1974.

Petry, Ann. *Harriet Tubman: Conductor on the Underground Railroad.* New York, N.Y.: HarperCollins Publishers, 1983.

Russell, Sharman. *Black Americans of Achievement: Frederick Douglass, Abolitionist.* New York: Chelsea House, 1998.

Schroeder, Alan. *Black Americans of Achievement: Booker T. Washington.* New York: Chelsea House, 1992.

Sterling, Dorothy. *Captain of the* Planter: *The Story of Robert Smalls.* Garden City, N.Y.: Doubleday & Company, Inc., 1958.

Taylor-Boyd, Susan. *Sojourner Truth.* Milwaukee, Wisc.: G. Stevens Children's Books, 1980.

To read original slave narratives, visit the University of North Carolina's website, Documenting the American South, at http://metalab.unc.edu/documenting.

Bibliography

Adams, Russel L. *Great Negroes: Past and Present.* Chicago: Afro-Am Publishing Company, Inc., 1969.

Adler, David A. *A Picture Book of Sojourner Truth.* Illustrated by Gershom Griffith. New York: Holiday House, 1994.

Blassingame, John W. *The Slave Community: Plantation Life in the Antebellum South.* Oxford University Press, New York: 1972.

Bontemps, Arna, editor. *Great Slave Narratives.* Boston: Beacon Press, 1969.

Bontemps, Arna. *Story of the Negro.* New York: Alfred A. Knopf, 1948; reprint, 1955.

Buckmaster, Henrietta. *Flight to Freedom: The Story of the Underground Railroad.* New York: Thomas Y. Crowell Company, 1958.

Cavanah, Frances. *The Truth About the Man Behind the Book that Sparked the War Between the States.* Philadelphia: Westminster Press, 1975.

Davis, Merlene. "Treatment of Slaves not quite what I was taught." *Lexington Herald Leader,* August 13, 2000.

Dedication of the North Carolina Highway Historical Marker for Harriet Jacobs. North Carolina Department of Cultural Resources, Historic Edenton State Historic Site, May 1998.

Douglass, Frederick. *Life and Times of Frederick Douglass.* New York: Gramercy Press, 1993.

Douglass, Frederick. *Narrative of the Life of Frederick Douglass: An American Slave.* Boston, 1845. Reprint, Anchor Books, a Division of Random House, New York, 1989.

Durham, Philip, and Everett L. Jones. *The Adventures of the Negro Cowboys.* New York: Bantam Books, 1969.

Ebony Pictorial History of Black America, Vol. I: African Past to Civil War. Nashville, Tenn.: The Southwestern Company, 1971.

Garrison, Webb. *Civil War Trivia and Fact Book.* Nashville, Tenn.: Rutledge Hill Press, 1992.

Garrison, Webb. "Georgia Couple Called Freedom 'The Greatest Christmas Gift'." *Atlanta Journal-Constitution.* Southeast Scrapbook column.

Garrison, Webb. "Uncle Tom's Cabin Fanned Flames of War." *Atlanta Journal-Constitution.* Southeast Scrapboook column.

Genovese, Eugene D. *Roll, Jordan, Roll: The World the Slaves Made.* New York: Vintage Books-Random House, 1974.

Henson, Josiah. *Truth Stranger Than Fiction: Father Henson's Story of His Own Life.* Introduction by Harriet Beecher Stowe. Williamstown, Mass.: Corner House Publishers, 1973.

Hughes, Langston, and Milton Meltzer. *A Pictorial History of the Negro in America.* New York: Crown Publishers, 1968.

Jacobs, Harriet A. *Incidents in the Life of a Slave Girl.* Edited by Jean Fagan Yellin. Cambridge, Mass.: Harvard University Press, 1987.

Katz, William Loren. *The Black West: A Documentary and Pictorial History of the African American Role in the Westward Expansion of the United States.* New York: Simon and Schuster, 1st Touchstone Edition, 1996.

Kent, Zachary. *The Civil War: "A House Divided."* Hillside, N.J.: Enslow Publishers, Inc.

Kimmel, Janice Martz. "Break Your Chains and Fly for Freedom." *Michigan History Magazine,* January/February 1996.

King, Coretta Scott, foreword. *Escape from Slavery: Boyhood of Frederick Douglass in his own words.* Knopf/Random House, N.Y.: 1994.

Krass, Peter. *Sojourner Truth: Antislavery Activist.* New York: Chelsea House Publishers, 1988.

Love, Nat. *The Life and Adventures of Nat Love.* University of Nebraska Press, 1995.

Miller, Edward A., Jr. *Gullah Statesman: Robert Smalls from Slavery to Congress 1839–1915.* University of South Carolina Press, 1995.

McKissack, Pat. *Booker T. Washington: Leader and Educator.* Hillside N.J.: Enslow Publishers, 1992.

National Park Service. *Underground Railroad.* Official National Park Handbook. U.S. Department of the Interior, Division of Publications. 1998; reprint, 1999.

Narrative of Sojourner Truth. Unabridged. Mineola, N.Y.: Dover Thrift Books, 1997.

Osofsky, Gilbert, editor. *Puttin' On Ole Massa: The Slave Narratives of Henry Bibb, William Wells Brown and Solomon Northrup.* New York: Harper Torchbooks, 1969.

Painter, Nell Irvin, editor. *Narrative of Sojourner Truth, A Bondswoman of Olden Time with a History of Her Labors and Correspondence Drawn from her* Book of Life; *Also a memorial Chapter.* New York: Penguin Books, 1998.

Powers, Bernard E., Jr. *Black Charlestonians: A Social History 1822–1885.* Fayetteville, Ark.: University of Arkansas Press, 1994.

Remembering Slavery: African Americans Talk About Their Personal Experiences of Slavery and Emancipation. Edited by Ira Berlin, Marc Favreau, and Steven F. Miller. New York: The New Press, in conjunction with the Library of Congress, 1998.

Roberts, Frank. "Historical marker honors slave who overcame the odds." *The Virginian-Pilot.* May 13, 1998.

Russell, Sharman. *Black Americans of Achievement: Frederick Douglass, Abolitionist.* New York: Chelsea House, 1998.

Schroeder, Alan. *Black Americans of Achievement: Booker T. Washington.* New York: Chelsea House, 1972.

Sherwin, Oscar. *Prophet of Liberty: A Biography of Wendell Phillips.* New York: New York University, 1943.

Sherwin, Oscar. *Prophet of Liberty: The Life and Times of Wendell Phillips.* Westport, Conn.: Greenwood Press, 1975.

Sterling, Dorothy. *Captain of the* Planter: *The Story of Robert Smalls.* Garden City, N.Y.: Doubleday & Company, Inc., 1958.

Taylor, Susie King. *Reminiscences of My Life: A Black Woman's Civil War Memoirs.* Edited by Patricia W. Romero and Willie Lee Rose. Princeton, N.J., and New York: Markus Wiener Publishing, Inc., 1992.

Taylor-Boyd, Susan. *Sojourner Truth.* Milwaukee, Wisc.: G. Stevens Children's Books, 1980.

Truth, Sojourner. *The Book of Life.* London: Black Classics, X Press, 1999.

The Life of Josiah Henson, Formerly a Slave, Now an Inhabitant of Canada. Narrated by himself. Boston: Arthur D. Phelps, 1849. Reprinted in 1965 by Uncle Tom's Cabin Museum, Dresden, Ontario, Canada.

Washington, Booker T. *Up from Slavery.* New York: Dell Publishing Company, 1965.

Winks, Robin W. Introduction to *An Autobiography of The Reverend Josiah Henson.* Reading, Mass.: Addison-Wesley Publishing Company, 1969.

Internet

African American Resource Center, Genealogy Forum: "Henry Walton Bibb—1815–1854." Http://www.genealogyforum.com/gfaol/resource/AfricanAm/Bibb.htm

"An Autobiography of The Rev. Josiah Henson (1789–1883)." Http://www.niica.on.ca/csonan/Josiah.htm

"Black Nurses in History." University of Medicine and Dentistry of New Jersey & Coriell Research Library. Http://www4.umdnj.edu/camlbweb/blacknurses.html.taylor

"Booker T. Washington National Monument Website." Http://www.nps.gov/bowa

"Brief History of Black Women in the Military." Http://www.womensmemorial.org/BBH1998.html

"Captain Robert Smalls." Http://www.abest.com/~cklose/caprsmal.htm

"Chapter XI: Literary and Professional Colored Men and Women"—Henry Bibb, Martin Delany and others. Http://www.libraries.wvu/delany/writers.htm

"Daily Journal 5—Uncle Tom's Cabin." Http://www.rims.k12.ca.us/ugr/1997/journals/day5.htm

"Documenting the American South: Electronic Slave Narratives." University of North Carolina at Chapel Hill Library. Http://metalab.unc.edu/documenting

"Election Methods in the South" by Robert Smalls. Http://www.furman.edu/~benson/docs/smalls.htm

"Ellen Craft." Http://www.womenofhistory.com/biolec.html

"Ellen and William Craft." Http://www.nps.gov/boaf/craft~1.htm

"Ellen Smith Craft 1826–1891." Http://www.gawomen.org/honorees/long/crafte_long.htm

"Frederick Douglass National Historic Site." Http://www.nps.gov/frdo/freddoug.html

"Fugitive Slave Law." Http://www.spartacus.schoolnet.co.uk/USASfugitive.htm

"Georgia Women of Achievement: 1996 Inductee Ellen Smith Craft." Http://www.gawomen.org/honorees/crafte.htm

"Great Moments: Josiah Henson." Http://www.ontario2000.on.ca/english/greatmoments/heroes/henson.html

"Harriet Ann Jacobs 1813–1897." Http://www.ncwriters.org/hjacobs.htm

"Henry Bibb." Http://www.spartacus.schoolnet.co.uk/Sbibb.htm

"Josiah Henson." Http://www.aalbc.com/josiah.htm

"Josiah Henson—Chapter 11." Http://xroads.virginia.edu/~MA97/riedy/henson.html

"Josiah Henson: We Lodged in Log Huts." Http://vi.uh.edu/pages/mintz/12.htm

"Martin Delany's Letters." Http://www.libraries.wvu.edu/delany/douglass.htm

"Nat Love, aka 'Deadwood Dick'." Http://africancowboys.com/html/9pg.html

"Nat Love." Http://www.in.net/~hartman/achievers.html#11

"Nat Love." Http://www.ukans.edu/heritage/kshs/people/afampeop.htm

"Pathfinder Rover Gets Its Name." Http://mpfwww.jpl.nasa.gov/MPF/rover/name.html

"Promoting Henson's 'Uncle Tom' by John Lobb. London, Ontario: Schuyler, Smith 1881. Editorial note and appendix A. African American Response.../@ebt-link?root+query

"Recent Acquisitions in African-American History." African-American Literature: Henry Bibb. Http://gopher.lib.virginia.edu/exhibits

"Robert Smalls." Http://www.beaufort-sc.com/history/smalls.htm

"Robert Smalls—Slavery and Emancipation." Http://civilwar.bluegrass.net/SlaveryAndEmancipation/robertsmalls.html

"Robert Smalls and His Environs"—*Beaufort Gazette.* Http://www.beaufortgazette.com/lifestyles/story/0,1465,82536,00.html

"Robert Smalls and the *Planter*." Http://www.almshouse.com/robert_small_and.htm

"Robert Smalls: United States Representative." Http://www.usbol.com/ctjournal/RSmallsbio.html

"Sojourner Truth: 1797–1883." Http://www.halcyon.com/ncorbett/sojourn.htm

"Sojourner Truth: A Biography." Http://www.iserv.net/~hsbc/sojourn.htm

"Sojourner Truth: 'Ain't I a Woman?'," Modern History Sourcebook. December 1851. Http://www.fordham.edu/halsall/mod/sojtruth-woman.html

"Sojourner Truth Quotations." Http://womenshistory.about.com/library/qu/blqutrut.htm?once=true

"Some Missing Pages: The Black Community in the History of Quebec and Canada." Unit 3: Fugitives for Freedom: Henry Bibb. Http://www.qesn.mesq.gouv.qc.ca/mpages/unit3/u3p69.htm

"Susie King Taylor." Http://www2./hric.org/pocantico/womenenc/taylor.htm

"Susie King Taylor: A Glimpse into the Life of a Civil War Contemporary." Http://www.kingtisdell.org/sktaylor.htm

"Steamship *Planter*." Http://history.navy.mil/photos/sh-civil/civsh-p/planter.htm

"The African American Journey." World Book Encyclopedia, 2001. Http://www.worldbook.com/fun/aajourny/html

"The Origin of Uncle Tom." Http://www.themarcusgarveybbs.com/wwwboard/messages/82.html

"Tuskegee Institute National Historic Site." Http://www.nps.gov/tuin

"US People—Robert Smalls." Http://history.navy.mil/photos/pers-us/uspers-s/r-smalls.htm

"William and Ellen Craft." Http://archive.msstate.edu/listarchives/afrigeneas/199712/msg00001.html

Index

A

abolitionist, 11, 21, 31, 34–36, 45–46, 54, 127
African emigration, 59
African Methodist Episcopal Church, 70
Akron, Ohio, 125
Alston, A., 105
American Beacon, 39
American Red Cross, 87
Anthony, Susan B., 127
Anti-Slavery Alamanac, 36
Anti-Slavery Convention, 21
Armstrong, Samuel, 70
auction, 2–3, 18, 27, 41, 44, 55, 75, 77, 118, 119
Auld, Hugh, 18
    Sophia (wife of), 17

B

Bailey, Fred, 13
    Betsy (grandmother of), 14
Baltimore, Maryland, 17, 31
Barton, Clara, 87
Battle Creek, Michigan, 130
Beaufort, South Carolina, 74, 80, 84, 87, 113, 115
Bibb, Henry, 49–59
    Malinda (wife of), 49, 53, 56
    Mary Frances (daughter of), 49, 53
Bibb, Senator James, 52
Big House, 16
Billy the Kid, 101
black cowboys, 98–102
black soldiers, 22–23, 80–90, 109–111
blockade, 85
Blount, Martha Hoskins Rombough, 48
Book of Life, The, 127
Booker T. Washington National
    Monument, 73
Booth, John Wilkes, 113
Boston, Massachusetts, 12, 36, 40, 46, 89
Brent, Linda, 38–48
    Jacobs, Harriet (true identity of), 38–48

buffalo, 99–100
Burroughs, Elizabeth, 64
    James (husband of), 64
Byron, Lord George, 36
    Lady Noel (wife of), 36

C

Cadwell, James, 127
Camp Shaw, South Carolina, 81
Canada, 7, 36, 53
caricature, 95
Castle Pinckney, South Carolina, 105
Charles County, Maryland, 2
Charleston Customs House, South Carolina, 31
Charleston, South Carolina, 26, 30, 31, 82, 86, 88, 103–4,
    107
Chase, Salmon P., 23
Cherokee, 58
Cheyenne, 70
Child, Maria, 45
Chisholm, J., 105
Christmas, 29, 33–34, 41–42, 44
Cincinnati, Ohio, 8
Civil War, 46, 64, 75, 94, 106, 127
    battlefield, 86
    nurse, 80
Cody, Buffalo Bill, 101
Coffin, Levi, 7
Cole Island, South Carolina, 109
Collins, Dr., 34
Columbian Orator, The, 18
Confederacy, 94
    soldiers, 82, 85
conjurer, 53
contrabands, 47, 109, 129–30
Cotton Exchange, 29
Cotton States and International Exposition, 72
cotton, 56–57, 121
Covey, Edward, 18

Craft Court (England), 37
Craft, Ellen Smith, 26–36
  William (husband of), 26–36
CSS *Virginia,* 111
Custer, George, 99

D

Dawn, Canada, 7
Deadwood, Dakota Territory, 99
Deadwood Dick, 91–102
Deeper Wrong, The, 46
Delany, Martin, 59
deserter, 61
Detroit Liberty Association, 49
District of Columbia, 56
Dodge City, Kansas, 98, 99
Douglass, Frederick, 11, 13–25, 72
  Charles (son of), 22
  Frederick, Jr. (son of), 22
  Lewis (son of), 22
Dresden, Ontario, 11
Du Pont, Samuel, 111
Dumont, John 120–123

E

Eaton County, Maryland, 13
economy, 8, 97, 98, 113
Edenton, North Carolina, 46
Emancipation Proclamation, 64, 66, 85
emigration, 59
England, 7, 36, 46
enslaved people, 50
Etowan, 105
extinct, 99

F

farmland, 56
fasting, 124
Ferguson, Washington, 61
field hands, 16
Fillmore, Millard, 35–37
Flint, Dr., 38–45
  James Norcom (true identity of), 48
Ford's Theatre, 113
Fort Johnson, South Carolina, 106
Fort McAllister, Georgia, 74
Fort Moultrie, South Carolina, 117
Fort Pulaski, Georgia, 78–79
Fort Ripley, South Carolina, 109
Fort Sumter, South Carolina, 106, 111, 113
Fort Wagner, South Carolina, 22, 82, 84, 86
Frederick Douglass Home and National Historic Site, 25
Frederick Douglass's Paper, 21
free blacks, 7–8, 54, 101
free state, 4–5
freedmen, 129–30
Fugitive Slave Act, 19, 34, 45

G

Gage, Frances, 126
Garrison, William Lloyd, 34–35, 127
Gettysburg Address, 32
Gilbert, Olive, 127
Glory, 82

Grant, Ulysses S., 25, 94–95
Great Exposition, 11
Great House, 16
Grest, Valentine, 75
Gridiron, John, 105

H

Hamburg, South Carolina, 87, 114
Hammersmith, England, 37
Hampton Institute, 69
  Normal School, 70
harassment, 42–43
Hardenburgh, (Belle) Isabella, 118–24
hardtack, 85
Hardy, Virginia, 73
Harvard University, 46
Hayden, Lewis, 35
Hayes, Rutherford B.
Henson, Josiah, 1–12
  Charlotte (wife of), 4
Hilton Head Island, South Carolina, 81, 83
Horniblow, Molly, 48
  Aunt Marthy (fictional name of), 48
house servants, 16
Hunter, David, 109
Huntington, Collis P., 72

I

Incidents in the Life of a Slave Girl, 40
Indians, 99
iron collar, 52
Ivens, Barkley, 34

J

Jackson, Abraham, 105
Jackson, Mildred, 52
Jacksonville, Florida, 82
Jacobs, Harriet, 38–48
  Brent, Linda (fictional name of), 38–48
James Island, South Carolina, 109
James, Jesse, 101
Johnkannaus, 42

K

Kentucky, 4, 52
King, Edward, 74
King, Martin Luther, Jr., 25
King-Tisdell Cottage Foundation, 90
Kiowa, 70
kitchen, 14
Ku Klux Klan, 37, 65, 67

L

League of Freedom, 36
Lee, Robert E., 94–96
Liberator, The, 34–35
Liberia, Africa, 59
Life and Adventures of Nat Love, The, 101
Life of Josiah Henson, The, 8
Lincoln, Abraham, 10, 13, 22–23, 65–66, 81, 109–10, 127–28, 130
Lincoln Memorial, 25
Little Bighorn, Montana, 99

Litton, Bruce, 4
Lloyd, Edward, 14
Love, Nat, 91–102
  Jordan (brother of), 92
  Robert Love (owner of), 92
  Sally (sister of), 92
Lowther, George W., 45
lynching, 115

M

Macon, Georgia, 27
Malden, West Virginia, 67
Manual Labour Institution, 7
manumission papers, 5
Maryland, 2, 11, 13
Massachusetts Anti-Slavery Society, 8
Massachusetts Units
  54th, 22, 82, 84, 110, 127
  55th, 22
master, 15
Masterson, Bat, 101
Matthews, Robert, 124
McKee, Henry, 113
McPherson, Dr. Josiah, 2
Metcalf, L. W., 82
Methodist minister, 5, 7
Michigan, 58
Miles, Mary, 59
mistress, 15
Montgomery County, Maryland, 2
Montgomery, Alabama, 56
Morris Island, South Carolina, 88
Morrison, William, 105
Mott, Lucretia, 127
  Lydia (sister of), 127
mulatto, 40
muster, 41

N

Narrative of the Life of Frederick Douglass, 21
Narrative of the Life of Henry Bibb, 59
Narrative of the Life of Sojourner Truth, The, 127
NASA (National Aeronautics and Space Administration), 130
Nashville, Tennessee, 98
National Anti-Slavery Standard, 45
National Era, 8
National Freedmen's Relief Association, 129, 130
naval history, 111–12
Neely, John, 119–20
New York, 20, 45
  slave laws, 122
Nickerson, Captain, 111
Norcom, James, 39, 48. See also Dr. Flint
Norfolk, Virginia, 39
North Star, 5
North Star, 21

O

O'Connor, Katie, 76
overseer, 1, 4, 16–19, 51, 55–56

P

Parker, Rev. Theodore, 36
Parris Island, South Carolina, 117

pass, 29, 76, 78
Philadelphia, Pennsylvania, 31–32, 112
Pierson, Elijah, 123
plantation, 14–15
Planter, 103–9, 112–13, 116
Port Royal, South Carolina, 84, 117
Portland, Maine, 36
poultice, 28

Q

Quaker, 21, 122

R

racism, 101–2
raffle, 99
rebel, 78, 82, 87, 94
Reconstruction, 98, 113–16
Red River Dick, 98
Red Shirts, 114
refugee camps, 130
Relyea, C. J., 103
Reminiscences of My Life in Camp, 85
Republican Party, 117
reveille, 86
Richmond, Virginia, 31, 56, 69
Riley, Isaac, 2
  Amos (brother of), 4
  Mrs. Isaac Riley (wife of), 11
Robinson, Marius, 126
Ruffner, Viola, 69
Running a Thousand Miles to Freedom, 36

S

Sandwich, Ontario, 59
Sands, Mr., 43–45, 48
  Sawyer, Samuel Tredwell (true identity of), 48
Savannah, Georgia, 30, 75, 76, 90
Sawyer, Samuel Tredwell, 48. See also Mr. Sands
Saxton, Rufus, 109, 113
Seabrook Island, South Carolina, 82
secession, 21
Shaw, Colonel Robert Gould, 82
Sherman, William Tecumseh, 74, 113
slave
  auction, 2–3, 75, 77, 118–19
  cabin, 14
  children, 59
  education, 37, 67–72, 75–76, 97, 109
  narrative, 40
  owner, 15
  rights, 2, 4
  runaway, 5–7, 19, 27–37, 45, 49–58, 103–7, 122
  state, 5
slave life
  female (harassment of), 42–45
  jumping the broom, 27
  living conditions, 15, 64
  marriage, 27
  plantation life, 13–17
  punishment, 1, 6, 13, 15, 16, 17–19, 28–29, 41–42, 51–53, 55, 58, 62, 75–76, 94, 103, 120, 122–23
  reading, 4, 7, 17–18, 28, 34, 40, 75–76, 80, 97, 125, 127
  religious life, 4, 7, 29, 34, 41, 50, 118–19, 123–25
smallpox, 80

Smalls, Robert, 103–17
  bribery charges, 115
  John (brother of), 105
  reward, 107, 109
  Robert, Jr. (son of), 112
  Sarah (daughter of), 112
  service in the U.S. Congress, 116, 117
South Carolina House of Representatives, 114
South Carolina Unit
  1st Volunteers, 80, 88–89, 109
Spanish-American War, 89
St. Simon's Island, Georgia, 78
Stanton, Secretary of War Edwin, 109
Stowe, Harriet Beecher, 8, 127
streetcars, 112, 128, 130
surgeon, 83

T

taps, 86
Taylor, Susie King, 74–90
  Russell L. (husband of), 89
textiles, 8
Tillman, Benjamin, 115
"Tom shows", 11
Trowbridge, C. T., 87–89
Truth Stranger than Fiction, 11
Truth, Sojourner, 118–13
  Baumfree (father of), 118–20
  children, 122
  lawsuits, 123–24, 130
  Mau-mau (mother of), 118–20
  speech, 126–27
Tubman, Harriet, 7
Tuckahoe, Maryland, 13
Turner, Nat, 41
Turno, Gabriel, 105
Tuskegee, Alabama, 70
  Tuskegee Institute, 71
  Tuskegee Institute National Historic Site, 73

U

U.S. Congress, 107
  Constitution
    13th Amendment, 64
  Federal Hospital, 83
  33rd Colored Troops, 80
Ulster County, New York, 118
Uncle Tom, 10. *See also* Josiah Henson
Uncle Tom's Cabin, 1, 8–10
Uncle Tom's Cabin Historic Site and Museum, 11
Underground Railroad, 7, 21
  agent, 7
  conductor, 7
  stations, 7
Union, 94
  soldiers, 84–85, 96
Up from Slavery, 65
USS *Keokuk,* 111
USS *Merrimack,* 111
USS *Monitor,* 111
USS *Onward,* 107

V

Van Wagener, Isaac, 122
  Maria (wife of), 122
Victoria, Queen (of England), 11
Voice of the Fugitive, The, 59

W

Wall Hollow, South Carolina, 87
Washington, Booker T., 61–72
Washington, D.C., 4, 11, 24, 31, 46, 127–28, 130
Welles, Secretary of the Navy Gideon, 107, 109
White, David, 52
Whitfield, Deacon Francis, 49, 56
Wilmington, North Carolina, 30
Windsor Castle, 11
wolves, 49
Women's Relief Auxiliary, 89
women's rights, 34, 125–27

Y

yankee, 76, 78, 92, 94
yellow fever, 22